Mount Pleasant Cemetery
Burial Index

Daniel B Durbin

Available on Amazon.com/books

ISBN: **1503019179**
ISBN-13: **978-1503019171**

DEDICATION

This index of burials is dedicated to the ancestors that came before us. This is an effort to preserve for posterity the footprints left by those that blazed the trails that we now easily follow. The corrosive winds of time would sweep away those footprints if they were not preserved. Tombstones eventually rot and decay as they succumb to the elements.

Knowledge of our past and how we arrived to "here and now" fortifies us for the journey to our future.

CONTENTS

ACKNOWLEDGMENTS

Thanks to the community of Big Reedy and the congregation at Mount Pleasant C.P. Church for their assistance in making this effort possible.

Thanks to my wife for her indulgence and acceptance of my passion for genealogy and her unwavering support.

1 - BURIAL INDEX

Mount Pleasant Cemetery is located in the northwest corner of Edmonson County, Kentucky near the borders of Grayson and Butler counties. The cemetery is adjacent to Mt. Pleasant Cumberland Presbyterian Church. The surrounding area is known as Big Reedy. Big Reedy is approximately 25 miles (40 km) due north of Bowling Green, or 13 miles south of Caneyville.

Directions: from Caneyville take highway 185 south for approximately 11½ miles. Turn right on highway 238. Go approximately 1½ miles, the cemetery and Mt. Pleasant C. P. Church are on the left. The old community schoolhouse still stands on the right side of the road.

The **Big Reedy** community is named for Big Reedy Creek, a tributary of the Green River which drains the watershed along the Edmonson County side of the current Butler and Edmonson County lines; the adjacent Little Reedy Creek drains a similar area of Butler County. John May and company recorded surveying 14,200 acres (57 km^2) on Big Reedy Creek on November 14, 1783. The community was established prior to the 1825 formation of Edmonson County in the section of Edmonson which was originally part of Grayson County. Many of the settlers were Revolutionary War and War of 1812 veterans, with a preponderance of settlers coming originally from Virginia, though many lived for several years in eastern Kentucky before crossing to Big Reedy.
http://en.wikipedia.org/wiki/Big_Reedy,_Kentucky

Mt. Pleasant C. P. Church was established in 1887 and the first community schoolhouse was built in 1896. The schoolhouse still stands, unused since 1940. The cemetery was in use much earlier, during the settlement years. The oldest legible death date in the cemetery is 1848. Some of the 70+ field rocks serving as headstones no doubt pre-date this "earliest date" to the late 1700's and very early 1800's.

There are 650 marked graves in Mt. Pleasant, 578 of which have legible tombstones. No doubt many original markers have been lost due to the ravages of time. There are at least 75 possible gravesites in the original old section (A) of the cemetery that are not marked.

The wrought-iron fence and entry portal to Mount Pleasant Cemetery are gone. However the serenity and beauty of the hillside cemetery have not lessened.

This index is a composite of a 1979 pen & paper survey and a 2014 photo survey. The 2014 survey assigned a Section, Row, and Plot number to each burial. This was done in an effort to assist in finding the individual grave of an ancestor.

The companion volume to this index, **_MOUNT PLEASANT CEMETERY AT BIG REEDY_** contains tombstone photos and genealogy information. It is available on Amazon.com/books.

Edmonson County, Kentucky

Mt. Pleasant Cemetery, located at Big Reedy.
The list was compiled by Howard W. & Deborah K. Jones May 9, 1979

Additions to the original list were taken from a photo survey by
Daniel B. & Sally J. Durbin completed in October 2014

Sect-row-plot	Surname	Given Name	Birth Date	Death Date
A-01-01	Bolton	R. M. *Ralph Morgan Bolton*	1924 Sep 07, 1924	Sep 16, 1924
A-01-02a	Childress	Ella Huff wife *Ella (Huff) Childress*	May 06, 1891	Jun 26, 1975
A-01-02b	Childress	Hubert F. husband *Hubert F Childress*	Jul. 01, 1889	Jan. 15, 1967
A-01-04a	Huff	Belle wife *Rebecca Belle (Woosley) Huff*	Mar 20, 1869	Mar 20, 1928
A-01-04b	Huff	Stanford husband *Stanford Huff*	Feb 24, 1859	Apr 28, 1945
A-01-05a	Vincent	Calvernia Willis wife of Gillis Vincent & mother of 10 sons, Roscoe, Beverly, Conrad, Elbert, Pat, Paul Raymond, Clyde, Haskell, Howell *Calvernia Ancenia (Willis) Vincent*	Dec 05, 1864	Oct 29, 1939
A-01-05b	Vincent	Gillis F *Gillis F Vincent*	May 10, 1864	Feb 22, 1948
A-01-06	Tomes	Zula Glendeen *Zula Glendeen Tomes*	Nov 27, 1917	Sep 13, 1921
A-01-07a	Tomes	James B husband *James Buchanan Tomes*	Aug 20, 1840	Apr 17, 1922
A-01-07b	Tomes	Rebecca wife *Rebecca (Miller) Tomes*	Apr 23, 1850	Jan 08, 1939
A-01-08	Oller	Cinthia F *Cynthia Francis Oller*	Apr 19, 1867	Jun 05, 1941
A-01-11	Tomes	Hubert son of C.F. & C. *Hubert F Tomes*	Jun 21, 1908	Jun 25, 1908
A-01-12a	Tomes	Cathern wife *Clarissa Cathern (Woosley) Tomes*	May 11, 1877	Sep 02, 1951

Sect-row-plot	Surname	Given Name	Birth Date	Death Date
A-01-12b	Tomes	Commodor P husband *Commodore Perry Tomes*	Sep 12, 1875	Dec 27, 1959
A-01-13	Woosley	John J son of J.C. & Martha *John Jack Woosley*	May 13, 1891	Dec 28, 1899
A-01-14a	Woosley	J. C. husband **John Campbell Brackinridge Woosley**	Sep 01, 1860	Apr 16, 1923
A-01-14b	Woosley	Martha Helen *Martha Helen (Woosley) Woosley*	Feb 02, 1866	Mar 04, 1938
A-01-15	Hardin	Charley **Charles Wesley Hardin**	Aug 16, 1897	Aug 11, 1899
A-02-01	Nash	Jeanetta Lucille Dau. Of E & A Nash age: 4 mts. And 2 days *Jeanetta Lucille Nash*	1928	1929
A-02-02	Johnson	Ersa Miller *Ersa M (Miller) Johnson*	Mar 30, 1909	May 19, 1975
A-02-03a	Miller	Maggie wife *Margaret T Maggie (Basham) Miller*	Feb 08, 1879	Apr 21, 1968
A-02-03b	Miller	Davis husband *Wesley Davis Miller*	Oct 16, 1874	Jan 05, 1944
A-02-04	Miller	Earleen *Earleen Miller*	Mar 17, 1929	Mar 18, 1929
A-02-05	Miller	Mary L. dau. Of W.D. & Maggie *Mary Levelle Miller*	Nov 18, 1901	Apr 01, 1905
A-02-06	Decker	Pheaba *Pheaba Decker*	Dec 10, 1814	Dec 27, 1905
A-02-07a	Bolton	G. M. husband *George Morgan Bolton*	Jan 08, 1863	Mar 22, 1931
A-02-07b	Bolton	Sarah A. wife *Sarah Adaline (Lawrence) Bolton*	Sep 06, 1865	Apr 22, 1945
A-02-08	Bolton	Avra E. *Avra E Bolton*	Jan 18, 1907	Jan 18, 1907

Sect-row-plot	Surname	Given Name	Birth Date	Death Date
A-02-09	Bolton	Eddie B. *Eddie B Bolton*	Dec 02, 1897	Feb 04, 1900
A-02-10	Tomes	Wiley F. *Wesley Wiley F Tomes*	Nov 17, 1884	Jul 07, 1957
A-02-11a	Tomes	Cynthia Wife *Cynthia Ann (Miller) Tomes*	May 08, 1861	Nov 06, 1946
A-02-11b	Tomes	I. D. husband *Indiman D Tomes*	May 08, 1858	Apr 24, 1940
A-02-12	Miller	Laura Ann *Laura Ann (Basham) Miller*	1854 Mar 11, 1854	1922
A-02-15a	Miller	Melissa A. wife *Melissa A (Woosley) Miller*	Sep 06, 1830	Nov 07, 1915
A-02-15b	Miller	Samuel husband *Samuel Miller*	Feb 06, 1826	May 18, 1916
A-02-16	Miller	Morgan husband of Candy Miller *Lewis Morgan Miller*	Nov 26, 1863	Sep 21, 1895
A-02-17a	Woosley	Samantha wife *Samantha (Huff) Woosley*	1867 Dec 26, 1867	1940 Jan 23, 1940
A-02-17b	Woosley	Lewis G. husband *Lewis Granville Woosley*	1866	1954 May 06, 1954
A-02-18	Woosley	Rosemon wife of John Woosley *Rosemon Rosie (Jones) Woosley*	Aug 05, 1832	Oct 31, 1892
A-02-19	Woosley	John husband of Rosemon *John Jack Woosley*	Jul 05, 1833	Nov 23, 1879
A-02-20a	Woosley	Susie W. wife *Susie Catherine (Woosley) Woosley*	Dec 20, 1869	Mar 22, 1934
A-02-20b	Woosley	Bluford W. husband *Bluford W Woosley*	Jun 07, 1865	Dec 05, 1951
A-02-21	Woosley	Addie wife of J. T. Woosley *Ruthy Addie (Wells) Woosley*	Mar 28, 1867	Mar 18, 1896

Sect-row-plot	Surname	Given Name	Birth Date	Death Date
A-02-22a	Woosley	George H. husband *George Hopson Woosley*	1866 Mar 16, 1866	1947 Mar 02, 1947
A-02-22b	Woosley	Meda wife *Elmeda "Meda" (Embry) Woosley*	1870 Jul 1870	1951 Aug 27, 1951
A-03-01a	Tomes	Essie P. husband *Essie Porter Tomes*	Sep 25, 1906	Jun 27, 1969
A-03-01b	Tomes	Stelsa M. wife *Stelsa M (Haynes) Tomes*	Jan 10, 1913	Dec 29, 1935
A-03-02a	Woosley	Glida E. Wife *Glida E (Tomes) Woosley*	Mar 08, 1901	Sep 29, 1998
A-03-02b	Woosley	Claudis R. husband married 10-20-1921 *Claudius Robert Woosley*	Aug 05, 1900	Aug 02, 1973
A-03-03	Woosley	Daughter of C.R. & C.E. Woosley *Infant Daughter Woosley*	Jan 08, 1928	Jan 08, 1928
A-03-04	Seaton	Ermal R. *Ermal Marie Rena Seaton*	Mar 10, 1930	Oct 14, 1931
A-03-05	Seaton	Estel G son of Roy & Thursey *Estel Guthery Seaton*	Feb 03, 1927	Jun 18, 1929
A-03-06	Seaton	Roy E. *Roy Estil Seaton*	May 20, 1902	Nov 27, 1931
A-03-07	Seaton	*Theresa Thursa (Miller) Seaton*	Nov 21, 1906	Jan 30, 2000
A-03-08	Huff	Ida Greturde *Ida Gertrude Huff*	Jan 31, 1911 Jan 31, 1911	Jan 31, 1911
A-03-09	Miller	Martha E. dau. Of A.D. & M.J. *Martha E Miller*	Aug 14, 1894	Sep 23, 1895
A-03-10	Miller	Mary J. wife of A.D. *Mary Jane (Jones) Miller*	Jul 12, 1875	Sep 03, 1895
A-03-11	Miller	Cornelius *Cornelius Miller*	Feb 01, 1885	Oct 17, 1957
A-03-12a	Oller	Ellen *Martha Ellen (unknown) Oller*	Sep 10, 1873	

Sect-row-plot	Surname	Given Name	Birth Date	Death Date
A-03-12b	Oller	Joseph T. husband *Joseph Terrell Oller*	May 31, 1870	Mar 31, 1923
A-13-13	Oller	Mary J. *Mary Jane (Woosley) Oller*	Jan 07, 1845	Mar 01, 1917
A-03-14	Oller	J. M. *James Marshall Oller*	Jun 28, 1837	May 23, 1915
A-03-15	Willis	Asbery husband of Christena Willis *Asbery Willis*	Oct 15, 1814	Jun 03, 1895
A-03-16	Willis	Melvin *James Melvin Willis*	Oct 06, 1845	Jun 13, 1917
A-03-16.01	Unknown	Block Marker *Unknown A-03-16.01 Block Marker*	Unknown	Unknown
A-03-16.02	Unknown	Stone *Unknown A-03-16.02 Field Stone Marker*	Unknown	Unknown
A-03-17	Miller	Rebecca *Rebecca Becky Miller*	Dec 20, 1875	~~May 14, 1969~~ **May 14, 1961**
A-03-18	Oller	Mrs. Lide wife of M. Oller *Eliza Lide (Miller) Oller*	Dec 20, 1866	Feb 17, 1917
A-03-19	Oller	Matchless husband *James Marshall "Matchless" Oller*	1865 Jun 25, 1865	1947 Mar 06, 1947
A-03-20	Goodwin	Lula Nash wife of Oren Goodwin *Lula (Nash) Goodwin*	Feb 26, 1885	Jun 15, 1939
A-03-21	Nash	John *John H Nash*	Jul 23, 1857	Aug 06, 1934
A-03-22	Nash	Margret *Margret E (Foreman) Nash*	Oct 03, 1858	Jan 24, 1903
A-03-23a	Lashley	*Texie Sue (Torrence) Lashley*	Aug 15, 1947	
A-03-23b	Lashley	*Charles A Lashley*	Sep 03, 1952	Jul 15, 2014
A-03-24	Embry	C. P. husband *Commodore Perry Embry*	Aug 16, 1866	Feb 22, 1923
A-03-25	Embry	Dina E. wife *Dina E (Woosley) Embry*	Jun 07, 1866	Dec 18, 1923

Sect-row-plot	Surname	Given Name	Birth Date	Death Date
A-03-26	Woosley	Martha T. wife *Martha Thomas (Woosley) Woosley*	Sep 23, 1871	Jan 21, 1924
A-03-27	Woosley	J. S. husband *James Samuel Woosley*	Feb 09, 1874	Nov 28, 1950
A-03-28	Woosley	Linnie *Linnie (Gross) Woosley*	Oct 08, 1901	Mar 01, 1979
A-03-29	Woosley	*Jannis Jann (Melton) Woosley*	Oct 02, 1955	Apr 16, 2001
A-04-01a	Lindsey	Darwin *Cuba Darwin Lindsey*	Jul 01, 1933	Oct 08, 1935
A-04-01b	Lindsey	Marjorie *Marjorie "Margie" Lindsey*	Feb 17, 1914	Apr 15, 1929
A-04-02a	Bolton	Leon Johnson wife *Leon Stanley (Johnson) Bolton*	Dec 16, 1895	May 16, 1975
A-04-02b	Bolton	George W. husband *George W Bolton*	Jan 16, 1893	Dec 22, 1976
A-04-03	Huff	Leudena wife of William *Susanna Leudena (Nash) Huff*	Oct 24, 1842	Oct 19, 1921
A-04-04	Huff	William husband *William "Billy" Huff*	Apr 01, 1842	Apr 04, 1908
A-04-05	Unknown	rock *Unknown A-04-05 White Stone Marker*	unknown	unknown
A-04-06	Bratcher	Clydus husband *Clydus Bratcher*	1911	1935
A-04-07a	Huff	George W. husband *George W Huff*	1894 Oct 30, 1894	1927 May 14, 1927
A-04-07b	Huff	Leva wife *Leva (unknown) Huff*	1901	
A-04-08	Unknown	Stone no markings *Unknown A-04-08 White Stone Marker*	unknown	unknown
A-04-09a	Huff	Dina E. Nash wife *Dina Elizabeth (Nash) Huff*	Feb 11, 1880	Oct 15, 1940

Sect-row-plot	Surname	Given Name	Birth Date	Death Date
A-04-09b	Huff	George W. husband *George Washington Huff*	Oct 01, 1881 Oct 01, 1881	Jan 10, 1973
A-04-10a	Huff	Allen husband *Allen Huff*	Aug 22, 1852	Jun 19, 1938
A-04-10b	Huff	Rebecca wife *Rebecca (Woosley) Huff*	Oct 09, 1855	Jul 20, 1944
A-04-11	Huff	Alfred son of A. & B. Huff *Alfred Huff*	Apr 13, 1879	Nov 04, 1895
A-04-12	Huff	William Albert Rev. Evangelist for 35 years *Rev. William Albert Huff*	Nov 15, 1877	Oct 16, 1955
A-04-13a	Willis	Volentine husband *Volentine T Willis*	May 24, 1842	Dec 25, 1925
A-04-13b	Willis	Serena Miller wife *Serena (Miller) Willis*	Nov 12, 1839	Nov 01, 1927
A-04-15	Oller	Julia A. aunt *Julia Ann Oller*	Mar 18, 1869	Mar 07, 1939
A-04-16a	Oller	Thomas M. father *Thomas Macentire Oller*	1859 May 09, 1859	1931 Jan 02, 1931
A-04-16b	Oller	Adeline N. mother *Rachel Adeline (Nash) Oller*	1856 Sep 15, 1856	1896
A-04-17	Oller	Morris M. son *Morris M Oller*	Mar 06, 1883	Aug 25, 1885
A-04-18	Oller	Lewis F. son *Lewis F Oller*	Oct 12, 1885	Mar 25, 1890
A-04-19	Oller	Gladys daughter *Gladys Oller*	May 15, 1896	Jul 05, 1896
A-04-21	Woosley	Venia Raymer mother of Ethel Lindsey *Luvenia "Venia" (Raymer) Woosley*	Aug 30, 1895	Dec 16, 1918

Sect-row-plot	Surname	Given Name	Birth Date	Death Date
A-04-22	Woosley	Lester *Lester Woosley*	Jan 11, 1895	Jun 28, 1962
A-04-23	Woosley	Syble Jones *Syble J (Jones) Jones-Woosley*	Sep 19, 1902	May 17, 1953
A-04-24	Woosley	Gracie Lee dau. of Lester & Gracie *Gracie Lee Woosley*	Jun 06, 1936	Sep 04, 1936
A-04-25	Woosley	Gracie *Gracie (Jones) Woosley*	Dec 18, 1915	Feb 13, 2002
A-04-26	Woosley	Carol Sue dau. Of Lester & Gracie *Carol Sue Woosley*	Nov 22, 1946	Sep 03, 1966
A-04-27	Woosley	Deanna Lynn dau. Of Lester Avon & Mary *Deanna Lynn Woosley*	Feb 15, 1951	Sep 03, 1966
A-14-28a	Woosley	*Mary L (Semon) Woosley*	Nov 07, 1917	Sep 13, 1997
A-04-28b	Woosley	*Lester Avon Woosley*	Jul 01, 1922	May 26, 2000
A-04-29	Woosley	Stephen Dale son of Kenneth & Joyce *Stephen Dale Woosley*	Oct 28, 1959	Aug 10, 1977
A-04-30	Woosley	*Mark L Woosley*	Aug 11, 1963	Oct 31, 1991
A-05-01	Nash	Irene Lewsader *Irene (Huff) Lewsader-Nash*	1890 Nov 20, 1890	1937 May 16, 1937
A-05-04	Duvall	Amos brother *Amos Duvall*	1922	1923
A-05-05	Duvall	Augustus Brother *Augustus Duvall*	1908	1922
A-05-06	Duvall	Sarah A. Mother *Sarah Angeline "Lina" (Farris) Duvall*	1884 Sep 08, 1884	1923
A-05-07	Duvall	Henry Father *Henry Warren Duvall*	1882 Nov 09, 1882	1923
A-15-08	Nash	*Emma (Williams) Nash*	Aug 03, 1847	May 22, 1927
A-05-09	Unknown	D. W. Stone *Unknown A-05-09 White D. W. Marker*	unknown	unknown

Sect-row-plot	Surname	Given Name	Birth Date	Death Date
A-05-11	Tomes	Andrew G. *Andrew G Tomes*	Oct 23, 1860	Jun 07, 1916
A-05-12	Toms	Rebecca 79 yrs.-2 mo.- 8 days *Rebecca (Baker) Toms*	Dec 04, 1819	Sep 26, 1899
A-05-13	Toms	Bluford 82 yrs.- 6 mo.- 28 days *Bluford Toms*	Feb 16, 1814	Sep 14, 1896
A-05-14	Nash	E. A. husband *Elijah A Nash*	Oct 05, 1863	Aug 25, 1931
A-05-15	Nash	Lucy A. wife *Lucy Ann (Goodwin) Nash*	Oct 11, 1868	Sep 13, 1919
A-05-18	Nash	Thomas *Thomas Nash*	Jul 27, 1887	Jul 27, 1887
A-05-19	Nash	Herbit *Herbit Nash*	Mar 26, 1886	Jun 05, 1886
A-06-01	Decker	Samuel Allen *Samuel Allen Decker*	Apr 04, 1922	Apr 13, 1922
A-06-02	Anderson	Senorah Roseline Tomes *Senorah Roseline (Tomes) Anderson*	Nov 24, 1879	Apr 24, 1938
A-06-04	Anderson	Ellie son of D. & S. *Ettie Anderson*	May 21, 1909	May 22, 1909
A-06-05	Anderson	Josephine wife of J. S. *Thelma Josephine (Tomes) Anderson*	Sep 01, 1876	Dec 18, 1918
A-06-08	Unknown	*Unknown A-06-08 Illegible Headstone*	unknown	unknown
A-06-09	Woosley	E. Sherly son of J.W. & Z.M. *E Sherley Woosley*	Aug 21, 1884	May 06, 1888
A-06-12	Woosley	Zilpham wife of J.W. *Zilphane M (Anderson) Woosley*	Dec 27, 1857	May 08, 1888
A-06-15	Forman	Marrie E. dau. Of C. & M. *Marrie E Forman*	Aug 21, 1877	Jan 02, 1893
A-06-16	Huff	Graften son of M.A. & N.C. *Graften Huff*	Apr 19, 1901	Apr 19, 1901

Sect-row-plot	Surname	Given Name	Birth Date	Death Date
A-06-17a	Huff	Nancy Candus wife *Nancy Candus (Miller) Huff*	Dec 17, 1869	Mar 24, 1929
A-06-17b	Huff	Marvel A. husband *Marvel A Huff*	Oct 08, 1865	Jun 15, 1937
A-06-17b.01	unknown	S. A. D. *Unknown A-06-17b.01 S.A.D. Marker*	unknown	unknown
A-06-18	Woosley	*Raymond Leon Woosley*	Feb 05, 1914	Sep 23, 1982
A-06-19a	Woosley	Ollie O. husband *Ollie Oscar Woosley*	Sep 18, 1884	Dec 17, 1945
A-06-19b	Woosley	Addie V. wife *Addie V (Huff) Woosley*	Nov 08, 1886	Jan 09, 1930
A-06-20a	Woosley	Mary E. wife *Mary Elizabeth (Simpson) Woosley*	Nov 21, 1840	Sep 09, 1913
A06-20b	Woosley	Merrel husband *Merrel Woosley*	Jul 19, 1838	Mar 02, 1906
A-06-21	Woosley	Elizabeth *Elizabeth (Oller) Woosley*	Oct 14, 1828	Apr 06, 1883
A-06-22	Woosley	G. W. *George Washington Woosley*	Feb 06, 1817	Jul 30, 1892
	Unknown	2 stones no markings	Unknown	Unknown
A-06-23	Unknown	*Unknown A-06-23 Illegible White Stone*	Unknown	Unknown
A-06-24	Unknown	*Unknown A-06-24 Illegible White Stone*	Unknown	Unknown
A-06-25	Woosley	Effa *Effa Woosley*	Jan 06, 1891	Jan 06, 1891
A-06-26a	Woosley	Stella *Stella O (Huff) Woosley*	Nov 22, 1885	May 14, 1954
A-06-26b	Woosley	T. J. *Thomas J Woosley*	Jul 12, 1867	Feb 02, 1946
A-06-27a	Huff	Commodore P. husband *Commodore Perry Huff*	1881 Sep 20, 1881	1955 Apr 05, 1955
A-06-27b	Huff	Nellie L wife & dau. Of Crit and Lou Jones *Nellie Lucy (Jones) Huff*	1884 Dec 11, 1884	1949 Oct 07, 1949

Sect-row-plot	Surname	Given Name	Birth Date	Death Date
A-06-28a	Gross	Elsie Huff wife & dau. Of C.P. & Nellie *Elsie Mae (Huff) Gross*	Jan 24, 1903	Aug 24, 1941
A-06-28b	Gross	Edward husband *Edward Gross*	Dec 30, 1898	Nov 29, 1960
A-07-01a	Tomes	*Ruby Cecil (Embry) Tomes*	Mar 31, 1916	Apr 01, 2003
A-07-01b	Tomes	*Hayward Pirtle Tomes*	Mar 12, 1913	Jul 19, 1980
A-07-02a	Tomes	*Kelvin Tomes*	Oct 04, 1934	
A-07-02b	Tomes	*Ottie (unknown) Tomes*	Jul 31, 1932	
A-07-04	Miller	Dona wife of Hallie *Caladonia "Dona" (Cummings) Miller*	Feb 15, 1899	May 06, 1931
A-07-05	Unknown	Willis stone broken most missing *Unknown A-07-05 Broken Stone Willis*	unknown	unknown
A-07-10	Jones	James Albert son of J.C. & L. *James Albert Jones*	Jan 29, 1879	Aug 29, 1881
A-07-11	Jones	Infant son of J. Crit & Nancy *Infant Son Jones*	Aug 06, 1882	Aug 08, 1882
A-07-12a	Jones	Loueller Woosley wife *Loueller (Woosley) Jones*	Jan 04, 1862	Jan 03, 1947
A-07-12b	Jones	John Crit husband & son of J.A. and Nancy *John Crittenden "Crit" Jones*	Jul 27, 1861	Feb 12, 1939
A-07-13	Cummins	Elizabeth wife *Elizabeth Jane "Eliza" (Woosley) Cummins*	Dec 11, 1855	May 03, 1892
A-07-14	Cummins	W. A. husband *William A Cummins*	Jan 29, 1855	Jun 15, 1877
A-07-15	Cummings	Edward son of J.A. & C.E. *Edward Cummings*	Aug 02, 1896	Aug 12, 1896
A-07-17a	Huff	A. husband *Alfred Huff*	Apr 22, 1857	Nov 13, 1919

Sect-row-plot	Surname	Given Name	Birth Date	Death Date
A-17-17b	Huff	Julia wife *Julia Ann (Woosley) Huff*	Apr 22, 1860	Jan 28, 1947
A-07-18a	Nash	Millard husband *Millard Nash*	May 24, 1878	Jul 12, 1945
A-07-18b	Nash	Oma Huff wife *Oma Wise (Huff) Nash*	Nov 08, 1880	Jul 10, 1930
A-07-19	Nash	Elvire J. wife *Elvira Jane (Woosley) Nash*	Nov 05, 1856	Feb 10, 1932
A-07-20	Nash	Samuel M. husband *Samuel M Nash*	**Jul 25, 1852**	**Jul 23, 1918**
A-07-21	Nash	Burtes dau of S.M. & E.L. *Burtes Nash*	Oct 17, 1884	Aug 08, 1886
A-07-22	Woosley	Zilpha Nash *Zilpha (Nash) Woosley*	Aug 11, 1893	Feb 03, 1933
A-07-23	Woosley	Silas Calvin husband *Silas Calvin Woosley*	Mar 15, 1877	Feb 09, 1944
A-07-24	Woosley	Minnie wife *Minnie M (Huff) Woosley*	Nov 08, 1879	Nov 04, 1911
A-07-25a	Miller	Palmon C. husband *Palmon Clatha Miller*	Oct 10, 1880	May 04, 1964
A-07-25b	Miller	Birdie wife *Bertha "Birdie" (Woosley) Miller*	Jun 19, 1880	Jan 14, 1929
A-07-26a	Woosley	Susan *Susan D (Nash) Woosley*	1844 Sep 05, 1844	1924
A-07-26b	Woosley	Joseph *Joseph Woosley*	1833 Mar 1843	1930
A-07-29	Huff	Lizzie Woosley wife *Elizabeth "Lizzie" (Woosley) Huff*	Oct 15, 1874	Mar 13, 1964
A-07-30	Huff	Leonard P. *Leonard Peter Huff*	Feb 04, 1872	Nov 20, 1917
A-07-31	Pawley	*Jo Ann (unknown) Pawley*	Sep 02, 1937	Sep 25, 2002

Sect-row-plot	Surname	Given Name	Birth Date	Death Date
A-07-33	Wilkins	Callie wife *Calverna Callie (unknown) Wilkins*	Apr 18, 1871	Feb 13, 1943
A-07-34	Wilkins	R. N. husband *Robert Newton Wilkins*	Sep 09, 1869	Dec 07, 1941
A-07-35a	Miller	*Lois A (unknown) Miller*	Sep 16, 1937	
A-07-35b	Miller	*William D Miller*	Mar 26, 1933	Jan 16, 1996
A-08-01	Unknown	*Unknown A-08-01 Illegible White Stone*	unknown	unknown
A-08-02	Tomes	*James Dolittle "Jimmy" Tomes*	May 23, 1944	Aug 10, 2003
A-08-03	Tomes	Jimmy Dwayne son of Jimmy & Betty *Jimmy Dwayne Tomes*	Aug 05, 1966	Jul 15, 1967
A-08-04a	Tomes	Jesse B. husband - married 3-26-1902 *Jessie Board Tomes*	1878 Jan 02, 1877	1965 Oct 06, 1965
A-08-04b	Tomes	Lura D. wife married 3-26-1902 *Lura D (Phelps) Tomes*	1878 Dec 09, 1878	1964 May 18, 1964
A-08-05a	Cummings	Andrew Casner husband *Andrew Casner Cummings*	Feb 14, 1889	Jan 16, 1926
A-08-05b	Cummings	Cora wife *Cora C (Toms) Cummings*	Jan 11, 1891	May 05, 1974
A-08-05c	Cummings	Gorden son *Gorden Cummings*	Sep 13, 1918	Jan 16, 1926
A-08-06a	Tomes	Frank husband *Thomas Franklin "Frank" Tomes*	1890 Oct 22, 1890	1958 May 11, 1958
A-08-06b	Tomes	Una wife *Eunice Bethel "Una" (Tomes) Tomes*	1893 Aug 25, 1893	1973 Nov 23, 1973
A-08-08	Huff	Alta wife of Ollie *Alta (Lee) Huff*	Sep 05, 1897	Mar 17, 1930
A-08-09	Tomes	Anderson *Anderson A Tomes*	Oct 19, 1848	Jul 22, 1931
A-08-10	Tomes	Julia A. *Julia Ann (Woosley) Tomes*	Mar 30, 1854	Jun 27, 1934

Sect-row-plot	Surname	Given Name	Birth Date	Death Date
A-08-11	Tomes	Wiley F. son of A. & J.A. *Wiley F Tomes*	Oct 27, 1876	Nov 25, 1879
A-08-12	Toms	Martha W. *Martha Washington Toms*	Oct 07, 1880	Sep 07, 1903
A-08-13	Toms	Infant of J. & C.A. stone broken *Infant Tomes*	Mar 25	Mar 25
A-08-14	Toms	Rev. Jasper husband *Rev. Jasper Thomas Toms*	Oct 15, 1840	Nov 20, 1908
A-08-15	Toms	Cintha A. wife *Cintha Ann (Woosley) Toms*	Nov 30, 1852	Nov 22, 1941
A-08-16a	Woosley	Judge husband *Judge Halsel Woosley*	Aug 12, 1884	Sep 24, 1976
A-08-16b	Woosley	Meda H. wife *Meda "Meadie" (Huff) Woosley*	Mar 04, 1882	Aug 27, 1931
A-08-18a	Miller	Arthur B. Nash husband *Arthur Beau Nash Miller*	Nov 01, 1832	May 02, 1926
A-08-18b	Miller	Artie Michie Tomes-wife *Artemecia "Artie Michie" (Tomes) Miller*	Apr 01, 1838	Apr 10, 1926
A-08-19	Miller	*Elizabeth "Liz" Miller*	May 09, 1864	Jul 10, 1927
A-08-20a	Huff	Precalla wife *Priscilla June "Precalla" (Bryant) Huff*	1864	1908
A-08-20b	Huff	Bedford husband *Bedford Huff*	1862	1941 Dec 12, 1941
A-08-21	Nash	Infant Dau. Of C. & B. Nash *Infant Daughter Nash*	Jul 30, 1900	Jul 30, 1900
A-08-22	Huff	Laura Bell dau. Of B. Huff *Laura Bell Huff*	Oct 16, 1881	Apr 03, 1882
A-08-23	Unknown	Field Rock *Unknown A-08-23 Field Stone*	Unknown	Unknown

Sect-row-plot	Surname	Given Name	Birth Date	Death Date
A-08-24	Unknown	Broken Stone *Unknown A-08-24 Broken Stone*	Unknown	Unknown
A-08-25	Unknown	Field Rock *Unknown A-08-25 Field Stone*	Unknown	Unknown
A-08-26	Raymer	Rob husband of Martha *William "Rob" Raymer*	Sep 06, 1863	Nov 18, 1896
A-08-27	Goff	Dona M *Dona M Goff*	Aug 21, 1893	Aug 04, 1952
A-08-29a	Huff	Mary Ann wife *Mary Ann (Willis) Huff*	1871 Nov 18, 1871	1943 May 10, 1943
A-08-29b	Huff	Sidney A. husband *Sidney A Huff*	1871 Mar 1871	1956 Oct 20, 1956
A-08-33	Miller	Walter E. *Walter Edward Miller*	1895 Sep 27, 1896	1935 Oct 21, 1935
A-08-34	Nash	Jesse James *Jesse James Nash*	1877	1973
A-09-01a	Miller	Lillie Mable wife *Lillie Mable (Hunt) Miller*	Jan 27, 1907	Nov 09, 1980
A-09-01b	Miller	Lloyd Wesley husband *Lloyd Wesley Miller*	Jan 16, 1905	Dec 17, 1971
A-09-06a	Woosley	Samuel husband *Samuel Woosley*	May 28, 1844	Aug 25, 1923
A-09-06b	Woosley	Mary J. wife *Mary Jane (Brooks) Woosley*	Jan 09, 1846	Jul 10, 1935
A-09-07a	Woosley	Benford R. husband *Bedford R Woosley*	Jun 25, 1883	Jul 08, 1963
A-09-07b	Woosley	Martha L. wife *Martha Lee (Woosley) Woosley*	Feb 06, 1887	Dec 12, 1935
A-09-08	Woosley	Shirley Gordon son of B.R. & M.L. *Shirley Gordon Woosley*	Jan 01, 1917	Feb 03, 1917
A-09-09	Tomes	Elizabeth *Elizabeth (Toms) Tomes*	Dec 22, 1832	Jul 18, 1906

Sect-row-plot	Surname	Given Name	Birth Date	Death Date
A-09-10	Toms	S. J. Most likely that James C and Elizabeth are parents. S J is buried between them. A daughter named Sarah Jane? *Sarah Jane Toms?* *S J Toms*	Sep 14, 1870	Mar 28, 1880
A-09-11	Toms	Jas. C. *James C Toms*	Jan 18, 1850	Jan 05, 1880
A-09-13	Forman	Sarah Jane dau. of C. *Sarah Jane Forman*	Jun 29, 1876	Jan 20, 1878
A-09-14	Forman	Paradine dau. Of T.W. & Polly *Pardine Forman*	Aug 09, 1870	Oct 24, 1872
A-09-16	Willis	Wiley husband *Wiley Willis*	Oct 15, 1845	Sep 23, 1875
A-09-17	Willis	Pheba F wife *Pheba F (Woosley) Willis*	Jun 01, 1849	May 07, 1925
A-09-18a	Woosley	Minnie H. wife *Minnie H (Huff) Woosley*	Mar 04, 1882	Nov 20, 1962
A-09-18b	Woosley	Volt husband *Volentine T Woosley*	Apr 25, 1873	Nov 25, 1960
A-09-19	Huff	Paradine *Paradine Huff*	Jun 29, 1865	Aug 06, 1920
A-09-20	Huff	Catherine wife *Catherine (Lee) Huff*	Jun 18, 1824	Feb 28, 1901
A-09-21	Huff	Nathan husband *Nathan Huff*	Jan 20, 1816	Jan 03, 1878
A-09-23	Miller	Pinkney husband *Pinkney Miller*	Jan 18, 1857	Nov 25, 1937
A-09-24	Miller	Alice J. wife *Alice J (Hardin) Miller*	Feb 14, 1851	Apr 11, 1880
A-09-25	Miller	Alice D. inf. Dau. of A. & P. *Alice D Miller*	Mar 31, 1880	Jul 21, 1880

Sect-row-plot	Surname	Given Name	Birth Date	Death Date
A-09-26	Miller	Ada B. *Ada B Miller*	Dec 18, 1897	May 18, 1899
A-09-29	Toms	Martha Dau. of S.J. & J.J. *Martha E Tomes*	Aug 23, 18?? Aug 23, 1892	Sep 01, 18?? Sep 01, 1892
A-09-30	Nash	2 Infant sons *Infant Twin Sons Nash*	Aug 31, 1904	Aug 31, 1904
A-10-30	Toms	Martha Ann wife *Martha Ann (Metcalf) Toms*	Mar 05, 1840	May 03, 1881
A-10-31	Toms	Redmon husband *Redmon T Toms*	Jul 25, 1838	Dec 08, 1907
A-10-32	Toms	*Bluford Toms*	Oct 15, 1865	May 03, 1868
A-10-35	Hardin	D. G. son of J.B. *D Gilbert Hardin*	Feb 07, 1890	Jul 07, 1890
A-10-36	Hardin	Nancy wife of J.B. *Nancy Catherine (Toms) Hardin*	Sep 26, 1861	Jun 27, 1890
A-11-35a	Willis	Cora wife *Cora Elizabeth (Ward) Willis*	Oct 12, 1879	May 19, 1950
A-11-35b	Willis	Daniel husband *Daniel Boone Willis*	May 16, 1870	Jun 12, 1927
A-11-36	Willis	Floyd husband of Senne *Floyd Willis*	Feb 06, 1901	Mar 20, 1926
A-11-39	Nash	Eva dau. of Hardie & Biddie *Eva "Evie" Nash*	Jun 24, 1904	Apr 11, 1923
A-11-40	Nash	Biddie wife *Lola Biddie (Crowder) Nash*	Jan 07, 1873	Feb 02, 1930
A-11-41	Nash	Hardie husband *Hardie Nash*	May 03, 1867	Feb 27, 1939
A-11-42	Nash	Charlie F. *Charles F "Charlie" Nash*	Sep 01, 1891	Apr 28, 1931

Sect-row-plot	Surname	Given Name	Birth Date	Death Date
A-12-01	Miller	Arvin son of Ova & Fannie *Arvin V Miller*	Jun 10, 1930	May 30, 1943
A-12-02	Miller	Mary M. dau. of Ova & Fannie *Mary M Miller*	Aug 03, 1932	May 30, 1943
A-12-03	Miller	Roy W. son of Ova & Fannie *Roy William Miller*	Feb 27, 1935	Nov 05, 1936
A-12-04a	Miller	Fannie *Frances "Fannie" (Lashley) Miller*	May 28, 1899	Jul 11, 1987
A-12-04b	Miller	Ova A. *Ova Vesterfield Miller*	May 27, 1895	Aug 12, 1970
A-12-06	Davis	James Lewis son of Hillard & Bytha *James Lewis Davis*	May 06, 1935	May 06, 1935
A-12-05a	Davis	*Bytha Woosley (Hampton) Davis*	Apr 13, 1912	Jan 13, 1993
A-12-05b	Davis	Hillard *Hillard Davis*	Oct 07, 1907	Jan 20, 1979
A-12-07	Davis	Hatieree dau. of T.J. & Eliza *Hattie Ree Davis*	Nov 18, 1902	Jul 02, 1905
A-12-08a	Davis	T. J. husband *Thomas Jefferson Davis*	Dec 08, 1858	May 25, 1935
A-12-08b	Davis	Eliza wife *Eliza (Woosley) Davis*	May 25, 1873	Jan 21, 1956
A-12-09	Woosley	Della son of T. & J. *Della Woosley*	Dec 22, 1885	Nov 05, 1888
A-12-10	Woosley	Terrel husband *Terrel Woosley*	Jul 05, 1840	Nov 11, 1919
A-12-11	Woosley	Nancy J. wife *Nancy Jane (Oller) Woosley*	Jun 28, 1840	Oct 23, 1882
A-12-12	Woosley	Jasper T son of T. & N.J. *Jasper T Woosley*	Jul 24, 1872	Mar 29, 1875

Sect-row-plot	Surname	Given Name	Birth Date	Death Date
A-12-13	Woosley	Mary E. dau. Of T. & N.J. *Mary E Woosley*	Oct 05, 1863	Sep 13, 1871
A-12-14	Oller	James *James B "Jamie" Oller*	Apr 23, 1799	Jan 20, 1875
A-12-15	Oller	George W. *George Washington Oller*	Jul 20, 1867	Jul 18, 1875
	Unknown	2 field rocks	Unknown	Unknown
A-12-16	Unknown	*Unknown A-12-16 Field Stone Marker*	Unknown	Unknown
A-12-17	Unknown	*Unknown A-12-17 Field Stone Marker*	Unknown	Unknown
A-12-19	Miller	Christopher *Christopher Miller*	Nov 11, 1801	Oct 05, 1858
A-12-22	Miller	Infant Dau. Of John & Rebecca *Infant Daughter Miller*	Oct 15, 1870	Oct 18, 1870
A-12-23	Miller	John husband *John Merideth Miller*	Jun 20, 1825	May 04, 1903
A-12-24	Miller	Rebecca wife *Rebecca (Woosley) Miller*	Sep 14, 1831	Jan 03, 1873
A-12-25	Miller	Samuel M. son of John & Rebecca *Samuel M Miller*	Mar 12, 1854	Dec 24, 1870
A-12-26	Miller	*William H Miller*	Oct 18, 1850	Oct 25, 1850
A-12-27	Unknown	Rock with lamb on top - not readable *Unknown A-12-27 Illegible Stone Marker*	Unknown	Unknown
A-12-28	Toms	James R. son of S. & P. *James R Toms*	Jan 08, 1865	Oct 16, 1867
A-13-01	Smith	Helen L. Daughter of L. & L. *Helen L Smith*	Nov 30, 1937	Dec 30, 1937
A-13-07a	Tomes	*Linda Darleen (Perry) Tomes*	Dec 15, 1946	Jun 18, 1984
A-13-07b	Tomes	*Dwight Travis Tomes*	Sep 21, 1946	
A-13-08	Woosley	Eva wife *Eva (Durbin) Woosley*	May 15, 1891	Nov 07, 1911

Sect-row-plot	Surname	Given Name	Birth Date	Death Date
A-13-09	Woosley	Valda husband *Valda Woosley*	Nov 20, 1889	Mar 28, 1976
A-13-10	Woosley	William husband of Eliza *William N Woosley*	Oct 22, 1863	Feb 18, 1902
A-13-14 New Stone "Woosley" should be A-21-26 Willis	**Willis** A-21-26 Woosley A-13-14	Nancy stone broken *Nancy Willis*	Nov 29, 1847	Dec 18, 1863
A-13-15	Conway	Lucian P. *Lucian P Conway*	Feb 02, 1884	Jun 09, 1884
A-13-17	Conway	Eveline wife of W.T. *Eveline (Willis) Conway*	~~Jan 25, 1840~~ Jan 25, 1849	Aug 11, 1882
A-13-18	Conway	Asa T. *Asa Thomas Conway*	Jul 16, 1873	Oct 18, 1874
A-13-21	Unknown	*Unknown A-13-21 Field Stone Marker*	Unknown	Unknown
A-14-24	Hayes	Hurshall T. son of R.L. & Dena *Hurshal T Hayes*	Aug 10, 1910	Aug 10, 1910
A-14-25	Wilson	A. W. son of T. & Dorthy *Anderson W Wilson*	Dec 10, 1868	Jan 20, 1890
A-14-26	Wilson	Dorthy wife of Tom *Dorothy "Dolly" (Nash) Wilson*	Jul 05, 1840	Jan 08, 1918
A-14-27	Wilson	Thomas *Thomas J Wilson*	Jan 25, 1834	Oct 24, 1872
A-15-01a	Tomes	Dorthy Huff married 3-15-1941 *Dorothy L (Huff) Tomes*	Nov 20, 1919	Jul 31, 1970
A-15-01b	Tomes	E. Sherman married 3-15-1941 *Emery Sherman Tomes*	Mar 31, 1917	Sep 24, 2003
A-15-02	Minton	*Helen P (Tomes) Minton*	Mar 20, 1908	Oct 05, 1993
A-15-03	Tomes	*Pirtle D Tomes*	Jun 30, 1910	Sep 19, 1996

Sect-row-plot	Surname	Given Name	Birth Date	Death Date
A-15-04	Tomes	Alvy *Alvy Tomes*	Jun 24, 1877	May 20, 1945
A-15-05	Tomes	Nora F. *Nora Frances (Horrell) Tomes*	Mar 17, 1879	Aug 25, 1963
A-15-06	Tomes	Jesse *Jesse Tomes*	Jan 16, 1904	Mar 28, 1926
A-15-08	Nash	Emma wife *Emma (Williams) Nash*	Aug 03, 1847	May 22, 1927
A-15-09	Nash	B. W. husband *Buford Walker Nash*	Dec 24, 1855	Jul 04, 1933
A-15-10	Nash	Edmon Ellwood son of B.W. & Emma *Edmon Ellwood Nash*	Nov 14, 1885	Sep 08, 1904
A-15-11	Nash	Infant dau. Of B.W. & Emma *Infant Daughter Nash*	Mar 28, 1888	Mar 28, 1888
A-15-12	Williams	Martha wife *Martha (Woosley) Williams*	Jul 01, 1808	Jul 13, 1877
A-15-13	Williams	John H. husband *John Haley Williams*	Jun 26, 1799	Jan 14, 1879
A-15-14	Woosley	Curtis B *Curtis Blakely Woosley*	1877 Apr 05, 1877	May 05, 1952
A-15-15	Woosley	Alberta *Alberta "Bertie" (Miller) Woosley*	Sep 15, 1877	Apr 02, 1945
A-15-16a	Woosley	S. C. Husband *Silas Calvin Woosley*	Nov 11, 1847	Jul 24, 1914
A-15-16b	Woosley	Millie wife *Mildred Millie (Nash) Woosley*	Feb 02, 1850	un 09, 1922
A-16-05	Webb	Kenneth M. son of Kenneth & Joy *Kenneth Michael Webb*	Oct 04, 1950	Oct 04, 1950
A-16-06	~~Tomes~~ **Raymer**	J. Pauline *J Pauline Raymer*	Oct 22, 1924	Mar 28, 1926
A-16-07a	Raymer	*Trulia (Tomes) Raymer*	Jun 03, 1902	Nov 03, 1981

Sect-row-plot	Surname	Given Name	Birth Date	Death Date
A-16-07b	Raymer	Charles E. 77 yrs. Old *Charles Estil Raymer*	1901 Feb 18, 1901	1979 Jan 15, 1979
A-16-10	Tomes	Infant Dau. Of G.K. & Wilma *Infant Daughter Tomes*	Aug 24, 1945	Aug 24, 1945
A-16-14	Huff	Owens son of A. & J. *Owens Huff*	Oct 26, 1893	Dec 22, 1895
A-16-16	Nash	L. F. *Demarcus Lafayette Nash*	Oct 09, 1841	Jan 13, 1906
A-16-17	Nash	Lousey wife *Louisiana "Lousey" (Phelps) Nash*	Nov 30, 1846	Sep 28, 1886
A-16-18	Nash	W.T. son fo L.F. *William Thomas Nash*	Mar 09, 1865	Sep 05, 1886
A-16-19	Nash	James Pendleton *James Pendleton Nash*	Dec 03, 1868	Jan 06, 1880
A-16-21	Nash	Mary M. *Mary M Nash*	Nov 11, 1870	Jun 09, 1880
A-16-22	Nash	Margaret wife *Margaret "Peggy" (Baker) Nash*	Aug 31, 1815	Oct 17, 1878
A-16-23	Nash	A. A. husband *Anderson Allen Nash*	Nov 02, 1814	Apr 22, 1889
A-16-24	Nash	Arthubeau son of A. & M. *Arthur Beau Nash*	Jan 20, 1844	Sep 23, 1866
A-16-25	Nash	son of Arthur Beau Nash *Emory Nash*		
A-16-26	unknown	Field Rock *Unknown A-16-26 Field Stone Marker*	unknown	unknown
A-16-27	Tomes	Hannibal son of J.B. & Rebecca *Hannibal Tomes*	Jan 20, 1874	Aug 18, 1901
A-16-28	Raymer	Clara C. dau. Of H. & M. *Clara C Raymer*	Oct 30, 1910	Jul 22, 1911

Sect-row-plot	Surname	Given Name	Birth Date	Death Date
A-16-29	Dotson	Ashti wife *Vasta "Vashtie" Blakely (Dotson)*	Jul 18, 1818	Jul 06, 1866
A-16-30	Dotson	James C. husband *James C Dotson*	May 11, 1822	Jun 14, 1895
A-16-31	Tomes	Hasibal son of J.R. B. and Rebecca *Hasibal Tomes*	Apr 22, 1875	Jul 26, 1914
A-16-32 = location **A-18-15.03** **UNMARKED**	Dotson	Barbra wife of J.C. *Barbra (Miller) Dotson*	Jun 27, 1835	Feb 18, 1925
A-16-36	Willis	Infant son of H. T. & C. *Infant Son Willis*	Jan 18, 1891	Jan 21, 1891
A-16-37	Anderson	Mary F. infant of G.W.A. & C. *Mary A Anderson*	unknown	unknown
A-16-38	Tomes	Clara infant of W.M.T. & Pheba *Clara Tomes*	Jan 04, 1920	Feb 04, 1920
A-16-40	unknown	stone *Unknown A-16-40 Stone Marker*	unknown	unknown
A-16-42a	Nash	Lucreca wife *Lucrecia (Willis) Nash*	Apr 17, 1847	Sep 30, 1918
A-16-42b	Nash	Daniel husband *Daniel Nash*	Nov 23, 1844	Apr 21, 1932
A-17-26	Toms	Thomas G. son of J.B. & B. *Thomas G Toms*	Sep 15, 1867	Sep 15, 1867 **Jan 1868**
A-17-27	Woosley	Infant Dau. of S.C. & M. *Infant Daughter Woosley*	Sep 15, 1867	Sep 15, 1867
A-17-28	Woosley	Elizabeth J. dau. of M. & M.E. *Elizabeth J Woosley*	Jan 22, 1861	Aug 15, 1861
A-17-29	Woosley	Infant Dau. of M. & M.E. *Infant Daughter Woosley*	Mar 01, 1868	Mar 01, 1868

Sect-row-plot	Surname	Given Name	Birth Date	Death Date
A-17-35	Willis	Infant babe of H. & M.E. *Infant Daughter Willis*	Aug 30, 1891 Aug 30, 1894	Aug 30, 1891 Aug 30, 1894
A-17-36	Willis	Infant son of H. & M.E. *Infant Son Willis*	Oct 18, 1887	Feb 24, 1888
A-18-01a	Tomes	*Dora G (Geary) Tomes*	Apr 11, 1915	Jan 04, 2014
A-18-01b	Tomes	*John Tomes*	Mar 03, 1906	Nov 11, 1983
A-18-02a	~~Raymer~~ Tomes	Elaine *Elaine Tomes*	Oct 07, 1931	Oct 07, 1931
A-18-02b	~~Raymer~~ Tomes	Leona C. *Leona C (Cummings) Tomes*	May 21, 1905	Oct 16, 1931
A-18-04	Johnson	*Sally Frances (Miller) Johnson*	Feb 12, 1912	May 05, 2005
	unknown	3 field rocks	unknown	unknown
A-18-08		*Unknown A-18-08 Field Stone*		
A-18-09		*Unknown A-18-09 Field Stone*		
A-18-10		*Unknown A-18-10 Field Stone*		
A-18-12	Nash	Marvel Jr. son of W.J.J. & Mary A. *Marvel Nash*	Sep 20, 1846	Mar 27, 1873
	unknown	3 field rocks	unknown	unknown
A-18-13		*Unknown A-18-13 Field Stone*		
A-18-14		*Unknown A-18-14 Field Stone*		
A-18-15.00		*Unknown A-18-15.00 Field Stone*		

A-18-15   **MEMORIAL TO UNMARKED GRAVES**

A memorial marker A-18-15 dedicated to all unmarked graves in Mount Pleasant was placed in a grotto surrounding the flagpole in the center of the old section of the cemetery. Listed are some of the individuals known or thought to be buried in Mount Pleasant

Sect-row-plot	Surname	Given Name	Birth Date	Death Date
A-18-15.01	Anderson	*Warren Elias Anderson*	Sep 24, 1863	Jun 28, 1934
A-18-15.02	Bolton	*John Riley Bolton*	Oct 24, 1800	1891

1979 survey had a J.R.B marker 2 graves outside of A-25-34 James E Simpson [1868-1879] marker not found in 2014 photo survey. 1979 Grave location A-25-36

A-18-15.03	Dotson	*Barbara (Miller) Dotson*	Jun 27, 1835	Feb 18, 1925

1979 survey had a Barbra Dotson [1835-1925] marker 2 graves to the right of A-16-30 James C Dotson [1822-1895], 1 grave to the right of A-16-31 Hasibal Tomes [1875-1914] marker not found in 2014 survey. 1979 Grave location A-16-32.

A-18-15.04	Carwile	*Nancy Catherine Carwile*	Aug 21, 1928	Aug 22, 1928
A-18-15.05	Miller	*Ova B Miller*	May 27, 1805	Apr 29, 1868

Sect-row-plot	Surname	Given Name	Birth Date	Death Date
A-18-15.06	Miller	*Sandra Pearl Miller*	Jun 08, 1944	Mar 25, 1945
A-18-15.07	Oller	*Cynthia F (Hunt) Oller*	Apr 19, 1800	May 06, 1849

Possible grave location A-12-16 or A-12-17 : There are several field stone markers in close proximity to her husband A-12-14 James B Jamie Oller [1799-1875].

Sect-row-plot	Surname	Given Name	Birth Date	Death Date
A-18-15.08	Simpson	*James Ward Simpson*	Oct 23, 1841	May 03, 1872

A marker for James Ward Simpson [1841-1872] was on a 1979 survey located next to A-25-34 James E Simpson, however, no marker was found during a 2014 photo survey of the entire cemetery.
1979 Grave location would be A-25-33

Sect-row-plot	Surname	Given Name	Birth Date	Death Date
A-18-15.09	Simpson	*Henry Lynn Simpson*	1814	Mar 03, 1859
A-18-15.10	Simpson	*Jesse S Simpson*	Oct 31, 1858	Sep 28, 1879
A-18-15.11	Toms	*Milly (Miller) Toms*	Sep 19, 1830	Jan 22, 1864

A marker for Milly (Miller) Toms [1830-1864] was on a 1979 survey located between A-23-18 Christopher Miller [1801-1858] and A-23-20 Christopher C Miller [1844-1870], however, no marker was found during a 2014 photo survey of the entire cemetery.
1979 Grave location would be A-23-19

Sect-row-plot	Surname	Given Name	Birth Date	Death Date
A-18-15.12	Woosley	*Infant Daughter Woosley*	Feb 22, 1884	Aug 15, 1884
A-18-15.13	Woosley	*Twin Boys Woosley*	Aug 24, 1848	Aug 24, 1848

MEMORIAL TO UNMARKED GRAVES
Markers placed in grotto around flagpole

Sect-row-plot	Surname	Given Name	Birth Date	Death Date
A-18-15a	Lee	*William Lee*	Feb 09, 1834	Aug 12, 1852

2014 survey - Grave headstone found A-26-28

Sect-row-plot	Surname	Given Name	Birth Date	Death Date
A-18-15b	Huff	*Nancy B (Pharis) Huff*	Aug 10, 1783	Sep 07, 1852
A-18-15c	Woosley	*James Joseph B Woosley*	Sep 18, 1808	Mar 09, 1864

2014 survey - Grave headstone found A-21-16

Sect-row-plot	Surname	Given Name	Birth Date	Death Date
A-18-15d	Simpson	*Marion Simpson*	Dec 16, 1853	Feb 27, 1861

2014 survey - a replacement marker found A-29-31. Note: name misspelled Marton

Sect-row-plot	Surname	Given Name	Birth Date	Death Date
A-18-15e	Woosley	*Lewis Franklin Woosley*	Oct 10, 1859	1931
A-18-15f	Huff	*Leonard Peter Huff*	1781	Apr 05, 1851
A-18-15g	unknown	*Aunt Lottie Negro Slave*	unknown	unknown
A-18-16	Hunt	Gemima wife of W. Hunt Gemima (Wommack) Hunt	Jul 12, 1811	Apr 15, 1876
A-18-17	Hunt	Willis *Willis Hunt*	Mar 10, 1805	Feb 20, 1878
A-18-20	Hunt	Eliza wife of G. W. *Eliza (Nash) Hunt*	May 18, 1858	Feb 25, 1885

Sect-row-plot	Surname	Given Name	Birth Date	Death Date
A-18-21	Nash	Elizabeth *Elizabeth "Betsy" W (Woosley) Toms-Nash*	Nov 16, 1820	Jan 24, 1924
A-18-22	Nash	Buford W. *Buford Walker Nash*	Dec 10, 1810	Jul 28, 1864
A-18-23	Nash	George Clinton *George Clinton Nash*	Apr 01, 1853	May 25, 1872
A-18-24	Bolton	Rebecca wife *Rebecca (Nash) Bolton*	May 30, 1847	May 16, 1878
A-18-25	Bolton	G. W. husband *George Washington Bolton*	Jan 26, 1845	Jun 12, 1917
A-18-30	Willis	Amanda wife *Amanda (Dotson) Willis*	Nov 15, 1825	Jun 12, 1879
A-18-31	Willis	Archible husband *Archibald Willis*	Dec 06, 1819	Apr 21, 1906
A-18-33	Willis	Dora dau. Of L.D. & R.J. *Dora Willis*	Dec 06, 1881	Sep 06, 1882
A-18-36	Oller	A. Lemia *A Lenia Oller*	May 05, 1881	Sep 01, 1899
A-19-10 A-19-11 A-19-12 A-19-13 A-19-14 A-19-15 A-19-16	unknown	7 field rocks *Unknown A-19-10 Field Stone* *Unknown A-19-11 Field Stone* *Unknown A-19-12 Field Stone* *Unknown A-19-13 Field Stone* *Unknown A-19-14 Field Stone* *Unknown A-19-15 Field Stone* *Unknown A-19-16 Field Stone*	unknown	unknown
A-19-17	Woosley	Lee wife *Leah "Lee" (Denton) Woosley*	Feb 01, 1843	Jun 09, 1922
A-19-18	Woosley	S. M. husband *Samuel M Woosley*	Jun 03, 1838	Aug 12, 1905
A-19-19	Woosley	*Greenville Woosley*	1838	Sep 09, 1863
A-19-20 A-19-21 A-19-22 A-19-23	unknown	4 Field rocks *Unknown A-19-20 Field Stone Marker* *Unknown A-19-21 Field Stone Marker* *Unknown A-19-22 Field Stone Marker* *Unknown A-19-23 Field Stone Marker*	unknown	unknown

Sect-row-plot	Surname	Given Name	Birth Date	Death Date
A-19-29	unknown	Field rock *Unknown A-19-29 Field Stone Marker*	unknown	unknown
A-19-39a	Williams	*Revil C (Brooks) Williams*	May 30, 1925	Aug 09, 1984
A-19-39b	Williams	*Hargus Williams*	Oct 13, 1917	Mar 04, 2002
A-20-06	unknown	S. W. rock *Unknown A-20-06 S.W. Stone Marker*	unknown	unknown
A-20-08	unknown	rock *Unknown A-20-08 Field Stone Marker*	unknown	unknown
A-20-09	unknown	Field rock *Unknown A-20-09 Field Stone Marker*	unknown	unknown
A-20-11	Huff	Matchless *Matchless Huff*	Feb 12, 1888	Sep 25, 1920
A-20-12a	Huff	Marth J. wife *Martha Jane (Woosley) Huff*	Jan 23, 1844	Feb 11, 1912
A-20-12b	Huff	Sidney husband *Sidney Huff*	May 19, 1847	Dec 31, 1890
A-20-13	Huff	Simeon G. son of S. & M.J. *Simeon G Huff*	May 27, 1875	Aug 11, 1876
A-20-14	Woosley	Thomas J. *Thomas Jefferson Woosley*	Dec 16, 1840	Dec 25, 1916
A-20-15	Woosley	Rebecca wife of Samuel *Rebecca (Blakely) Woosley*	Oct 25, 1808	Jul 17, 1890
A-20-16	Woosley	Samuel husband of Rebecca *Samuel Woosley*	Dec 23, 1802	Aug 08, 1865
A-20-17	Toms	*Infant Son Toms*	Oct 04, 1852	Oct 04, 1852
A-20-18	Toms	*Elias W Toms*	Jan 10, 1856	Mar 16, 1859
A-20-21	unknown	*Unknown A-20-21 Field Stone Marker*	unknown	unknown
A-20-24	Nash	*Arthur Beau Nash Jr.*	Apr 06, 1818	Feb 19, 1862
A-20-25	Jones	*Thomas Jones*	Aug 18, 1834	Oct 19, 1858
A-20-26	Jones	*Mary (unknown) Jones*	Abt. 1835	unknown
A-20-28a	Willis	Rebecca *Rebecca A (Nash) Willis*	Jan 20, 1849	May 10, 1916

Sect-row-plot	Surname	Given Name	Birth Date	Death Date
A-20-28b	Willis	G. M. *George Melvin Willis*	Aug 12, 1849	Jul 10, 1916
A-20-31	Willis	Cader son of A. & C.W. *Cader Willis*	May 16, 1861	May 16, 1861
A-20-33	Minton	Ollevi dau. *Ollevi Minton*	Dec 26, 1862	Mar 22, 1864
A-20-35	Cummins	S. O. *Squire D Cummins*	Jun 24, 1835	Dec 11, 1865
A-20-36	Cummins	Ruth A. B. *Rutha B Cummins*	Feb 23, 1844	Jul 09, 1867
A-20-39	unknown	Field rock *Unknown A-20-39 Field Stone Marker*	unknown	unknown
A-20-40	Jones	Jacob D. *Jacob D Jones*	Oct 22, 1846	Sep 18, 1920
A-20-43a	Williams	Connard husband *Connard Williams*	1923 Nov 22, 1923	Jan 08, 1969
A-20-43b	Williams	Irene wife *Irene (Swift) Williams*	1924	1957
A-20-44	Swift	*Victoria (Embry) Swift*	Apr 04, 1904	May 01, 1983
A-21-16 UNMARKED Grotto				
A-18-15c	Woosley	Joseph B. 56 yrs., 5 mo., & 20 days *James Joseph B Woosley*	Sep 18, 1800	Mar 09, 1861
A-21-17	Huff	Sarah E. dau of Wm. Huff *Sarah E Huff*	Sep 18, 1872	Dec 27, 1884
A-21-18	Huff	James son of W. & L. *James Huff*	Nov 14, 1871	Jan 31, 1873
A-21-19	Huff	Pendleton son of W. & L. *Pendleton Huff*	Nov 03, 1862	Aug 17, 1864
A-21-20	Nash	Milly 74 yrs., 6 mo., 25 days *Milly (Toms) Nash*	Sep 14, 1784	Jul 08, 1859

Sect-row-plot	Surname	Given Name	Birth Date	Death Date
A-21-21	Nash	Arthur B. 74 yrs., 5 mo., 27 days *Arthur Beau Nash*	Oct 10, 1780	Apr 07, 1854
A-21-23	Woosley	Robert son of Dr. J. H. *Robert A Woosley*	Dec 25, 1851	Aug 08, 1858
A-21-24	Willis	Elizabeth wife *Elizabeth Tolbert (Miller) Willis*	Sep 04, 1826	Jun 16, 1882
A-21-25	Willis	Daniel husband *Daniel Willis*	Jul 25, 1823	Sep 15, 1852
A-21-26	Willis	Nancy dau. of D. & E. *Nancy Willis*	Nov 29, 1847	Dec 18, 1863
A-21-27	Jones	Nancy Elizabeth dau. Of D. & E. Willis *Nancy Elizabeth Jones*	Apr 08, 1867	Sep 30, 1868
A-21-28	Jones	Manerva wife of J. Jones dau. Of D. & E. Willis *Manerva (Willis) Jones*	Oct 14, 1846	Apr 14, 1880
A-21-30	Willis	A. A. *Anderson A Willis*	Jan 03, 1871	Jun 05, 1888
A-21-32	unknown	Field rock *Unknown A-21-32 Field Stone Marker*	unknown	unknown
A-21-34	unknown	R.B.E. rock *Unknown A-21-34 RBE Stone Marker*	unknown	unknown
A-21-36	Preston	Margaret E. wife of JNO *Margaret E (Willis) Preston*	Dec 15, 1872	Aug 26, 1892
A-20-37	Geary	Daniel son of A. & L. *Daniel Geary*	Sep 28, 1912	Oct 01, 1914
A-21-38a	Geary	Rev. Azro husband *Rev. Azro Geary*	Mar 31, 1892	Jun 15, 1966
A-3-21-38b	Geary	Lina wife *Perlina "Lina" (Willis) Geary*	Sep 25, 1873	Feb 03, 1937
A-21-39a	Williams	Josie wife *Josephine "Josie" (Huff) Williams*	1884	1967

Sect-row-plot	Surname	Given Name	Birth Date	Death Date
A-21-39b	Wiliams	Calvin husband *John Calvin Williams*	Jan 29, 1878	Mar 05, 1942
A-21-40	Williams	Goebel *William Goebel Williams*	Feb 09, 1903	Oct 09, 1973
A-21-41a	Bryant	John husband *John B Bryant*	May 10, 1883	Jan 30, 1976
A-21-41b	Bryant	Mollie wife *Mollie (Huff) Bryant*	Sep 25, 1886	Feb 14, 1974
A-22-16	Nash	*James B Warren Nash*	Apr 02, 1841	May 01, 1878
A-22-17	Nash	*Nancy Hundley (Miller) Nash*	Jun 10, 1834	May 20, 1877
A-22-18	unknown	*Unknown A-22-18 Field Stone Marker*	unknown	unknown
A-22-22	Nash	*William Warren Nash*	Jul 14, 1863	Sep 28, 1864
A-22-23	Nash	*Mary Polly (Willis) Nash*	May 16, 1824	Sep 12, 1855
A-22-24	Oller	*Lucinda (Johnson) Oller-Willis*	Jul 21, 1832	Jun 28, 1863
A-22-25	Oller	*Holy Matchless Oller*	Mar 23, 1829	Sep 09, 1854
A-22-26	unknown	*Unknown A-22-26 Field Stone Marker*	unknown	unknown
A-22-27	unknown	*Unknown A-22-27 Field Stone Marker*	unknown	unknown
A-22-28	unknown	*Unknown A-22-28 Field Stone Marker*	unknown	unknown
A-22-31	unknown	*Unknown A-22-31 Field Stone Marker*	unknown	unknown
A-22-32	unknown	*Unknown A-22-32 Field Stone Marker*	unknown	unknown
A-22-37	Willis	Charles Ray son of W. & R. *Charles Ray Willis*	Jan 24, 1925	Jan 30, 1925
A-22-42a	Basham	*Campbell Olis Basham*	Nov 18, 1918	Mar 08, 2008
A-22-42b	Basham	*Nova (Woosley) Basham*	Dec 04, 1917	Nov 09, 2001
A-23-16	Willis	Calafornia dau. Of V.T. & S. *Susan California Willis*	Dec 18, 1867	Nov 19, 1870
A-23-17	Miller	Nancy H. *Nancy Hundley (Nash) Miller*	Feb 10, 1805	Apr 29, 1868
A-23-18 A-12-19 Duplicate Stone	Miller	Christopher *Christopher Miller*	Nov 11, 1801	Oct 05, 1858

Sect-row-plot	Surname	Given Name	Birth Date	Death Date
A-23-18b UNMARKED A-18-15.11	Tombs	Milly *Milly (Miller) Toms*	Sep 19, 1830	Jan 22, 1864
A-23-19	Tomes	J *J Tomes*	1830	1864
A-23-20	Miller	Christopher C **Christopher C Miller**	Dec 29, 1841 **Dec 29, 1844**	Mar 20, 1870
A-23-21	Anderson	L. A. husband *Lewis Andrew Anderson*	Feb 08, 1829	Mar 19, 1918
A-23-22	Anderson	Permelia wife *Mary Permelia (Nash) Anderson*	Dec 09, 1835	Apr 29, 1877
A-23-23	Anderson	Infant dau. Of L.A. & Permelia *Infant Daughter Anderson*	Aug 1859	Aug 1859
A-23-24	Anderson	Dartha *Dartha Anderson*	Mar 03, 1865	Jul 08, 1865
A-23-25 A-23-26	unknown	2 Field rocks *Unknown A-23-25 Field Stone Marker* *Unknown A-23-26 Field Stone Marker*	unknown	unknown
A-23-27	Anderson	Sharles *Charles C Anderson*	Apr 23, 1841	Mar 18 (?)
A-23-28	unknown	1 Field rock *Unknown A-23-28 Field Rock Marker*	unknown	unknown
A-23-29	Anderson	A. B. *Arthur B Anderson*	1832 Apr 29, 1832	Mar 15, 1852
A-23-31	unknown	Field rock *Unknown A-23-31 Field Rock Marker*	unknown	unknown
A-23-32	Anderson	Volentine husband of C. *Valentine Anderson*	Sep 30, 1830	Dec 01, 1876
A-23-33	Embry	Larence E. son of V.C. & C.A. *Clarence Embry*	Sep 12, 1908	Oct 26, 1908
A-23-34a	Embry	Callie wife **Callie (Ellis) Embry**	1881 Aug 1881	Jan 19, 1965
A-23-34b	Embry	Vergil C. husband *Vergil Crit Embry*	1876 Jun 19, 1876	1941

Sect-row-plot	Surname	Given Name	Birth Date	Death Date
A-24-18	unknown	Unknown A-24-18 Field Stone Marker	unknown	unknown
A-24-19	Miller	Rachel *Rachel (Musick) Miller*	Jul 04, 1808	Nov 24, 1883
A-24-20	Miller	Abraham K. *Abraham Kingery Miller*	Nov 23, 1804 Nov 23, 1801	Nov 25, 1888
A-24-21 A-24-22	unknown	2 field rocks *Unknown A-24-21 Field Stone Marker* *Unknown A-24-22 Field Stone Marker*	unknown	unknown
A-24-23	unknown	J.B. *Josiah Bolton? Footstone?*	unknown 1840	unknown 1862
A-24-24	Bolton	Hale *Haile Hail Bolton*	Feb 12, 1813	Aug 10, 1889
A-24-25	Bolton	Dinall wife *Dinah (Woosley) Bolton*	Dec 25, 1815	Dec 29, 1883
A-24-26	Bolton	Dr. B. L. *Dr. Beverly L Bolton*	Jun 01, 1856	Feb 22, 1880
A-24-27	Bolton	James M. *James M Bolton*	Apr 18, 1843	Sep 03, 1858
A-24-27	unknown	J.M.B. *James M Bolton? Footstone?*	unknown Apr 18, 1843	unknown Sep 03, 1858
A-24-27a	Bolton	James Riley *John Riley Bolton*	Oct 24, 1850	Jan 28, 1857
A-24-27a	unknown	J.R.B. *John Riley Bolton? Footstone?*	unknown Oct 24, 1800	unknown 1891
A-24-28	Bolton	Julyan *Julyan Bolton*	Nov 04, 1848	Sep 12, 1854
A-24-29	Unknown	(name not readable) *Unknown A-24-29 Illegible Marker*	Apr 06, 1861	1869
A-24-30	Hunt	Julia Ann *Julia Ann Hunt*	Jan 01, 1863	Jan 01, 1863
A-24-31a A-24-31b	unknown	2 field rocks *Unknown A-24-31a Field Stone Marker* *Unknown A-24-31b Field Stone Marker*	unknown	unknown
A-24-32	Hunt	George *George Hunt*	Jan 03, 1868	Apr 16, 1890
A-23-33	Hunt	*George W Hunt*	May 18, 1838	Feb 27, 1881
A-24-34	Bolton	Valentine son of S.H. & S.A. *Valentine Bolton*	Aug 12, 1881	Sep 15, 1886

Sect-row-plot	Surname	Given Name	Birth Date	Death Date
A-24-35a	Bolton	Sarah Ann wife *Sarah Ann (Foreman) Bolton*	Dec 10, 1860	Aug 09, 1930
A-24-35b	Bolton	S. H. husband *Samuel Hale Bolton*	Apr 04, 1853	Mar 22, 1931
A-24-36	Bolton	Lewis F. husband *Lewis Franklin Bolton*	Sep 23, 1837	Jun 17, 1915
A-24-37	Bolton	Mary V. Wife *Mary Virginia (Thacker) Bolton*	Dec 10, 1847	Jul 11, 1921
A-24-38	Mattingly	*James Gordon Mattingly*	Dec 04, 1915	Nov 29, 2005
A-25-33 UNMARKED A-18-15.08	Simpson	James W husband of Joanna P (31 yrs., 9 mo., 23 days) *James Ward Simpson*	~~May 03, 1872~~ **Oct 23, 1841**	 **May 03, 1872**
A-25-34	Simpson	J. E. *James E Simpson*	Oct 31, 1868	Sep 28, 1879
A-26-18	Miller	Elranor dau. Of M. & L *Eleanor Miller*	Dec 10, 1870	Feb 23, 1871
A-26-19a	Miller	Argalas twin son of M. & L. *Argalas Miller*	Nov 30, 1869	Feb 01, 1870
A-26-19b	Miller	Silvanus S twin son of M. & L. *Silvanus S Miller*	Nov 30, 1869	Feb 05, 1870
A-26-20	Nash	Thurv *Thurv Nash*	Apr , (?) Cir 1850	
A-26-22	Lee	Field rock *Unknown A-24-22 Field Stone Marker*	unknown	unknown
A-26-24	Lee	V. L. *Unknown A-26-24 V L Stone Marker*		
A-26-26	Lee	Viola Y *Viola Y Lee*	May 18, 1866	Mar 11, 1868
A-26-28 A-18-15a UNMARKED Grotto	Lee	Wm. *William Lee*	 Feb 09, 1834	 Aug 12, 1852

Sect-row-plot	Surname	Given Name	Birth Date	Death Date
A-26-29	Lee	Barnett husband *Barnett Lee*	May 10, 1795	Dec 09, 1869
A-26-30	Lee	Sarah wife *Sarah (Parrott) Lee*	Dec 15, 1800	May 29, 1881
A-26-31	unknown	Field rock *Unknown A-26-31 Field Stone Marker*	unknown	unknown
A-27-19	unknown	L. L. S. *Unknown A-27-19 Stone Marker*	unknown	unknown
A-27-20	Simpson	Azel *Azel Simpson*	Feb 01, 1787	Jul 06, 1863
A-27-21a	Simpson	Martha E. wife *Martha E (Huff) Simpson*	Mar 03, 1845	Mar 11, 1911
A-27-21b	Simpson	John E. husband *John E Simpson*	Apr 21, 1844	Sep 05, 1869
A-27-22	Simpson	Adaline dau. Of John & Martha *Adaline Simpson*	May 09, 1869	Nov 23, 1885
A-27-23	Simpson	Addieville *Addieville Simpson*	May 15, 1867	Jun 14, 1944
A-27-24 A-27-26 A-27-31	unknown	3 Field rocks *Unknown A-27-24 Field Stone Marker* *Unknown A-27-26 Field Stone Marker* *Unknown A-27-31 Field Stone Marker*	unknown	unknown
A-28-39	Tapscott	*Delphia Lucille (Lindsey) Tapscott*	Dec 05, 1945	Feb 20, 1993
A-28-40	Reddish	*Mittie Crystal (Hultz) Reddish*	Nov 28, 1895	Nov 04, 1969
A-29-30	Simpson	Henry *Henry Simpson* Probable son of Azel - grave next to Marion another son	18?? circa 1850	
A-29-31 UNMARKED Grotto A-18-15d	Simpson	Marton *Marion Simpson*	Dec 16, 1853	Feb 27, 1861

Sect-row-plot	Surname	Given Name	Birth Date	Death Date
		Mt. Pleasant cemetary on other (north) side of the church		
	Surname	Given Name	Birth Date	Death Date
B-01-01a	Huff	*Herbert Huff*	Jan 21, 1897	Jun 05, 1988
B-01-01b	Huff	Setta Tomes *Stella Setta (Tomes) Huff*	Oct 02, 1898	Apr 26, 1979
B-01-02a	Huff	Roscoe husband - Married 1-03-1913 *Roscoe Huff*	Jan 18, 1891	Jan 19, 1961
B-01-02b	Huff	Anthia wife *Anthia Gerter (Huff) Huff*	1891	Jan 01, 1970
B-01-03b	Huff	Hazel Dawn wife *Hazel Dawn (Clark) Huff*	Jul 24, 1920	Jul 26, 1972
B-01-03a	Huff	Denby husband *Denby Huff*	May 12, 1924	Jul 31, 2009
B-01-04a	Huff	Dr. Chester husband - married 9-18-1912 *Dr. Chester Huff*	Apr 22, 1889	Feb 01, 1973
B-01-04b	Huff	Blanche wife *Blanche Rebecca (Huff) Huff*	Nov 26, 1895	Dec 06, 1984
B-01-05	Huff	*Madolyn C Huff*	Apr 15, 1947	
B-01-06	Huff	*Gertrude (Whoberry) Huff*	Jan 12, 1922	Apr 12, 2012
B-01-07a	Woosley	*Eric Richard Woosley*	Oct 29, 1962	
B-01-07b	Woosley	*Melinda Christine (Huff) Woosley*	Nov 23, 1963	May 10, 2008
B-02-01a	Woosley	*McKelvy Woosley*	Oct 03, 1922	Aug 01, 2007
B-02-01b	Woosley	*Frieda (Childress) Woosley*	Jul 20, 1924	Aug 05, 1987
B-02-02a	Smith	*Larry Smith*	Dec 12, 1948	
B-02-02b	Smith	*Joann (Woosley) Smith*	Oct 12, 1950	Feb 05, 2012
B-02-03a	Morse	*Ownard D Morse*	Apr 05, 1904	Oct 01, 1982
B-02-03b	Morse	*Delphia W (Woosley) Morse*	Oct 03, 1905	Sep 29, 1991
B-02-04a	Raymer	*Berthel Raymer*	Mar 27, 1924	Apr 08, 1983
B-02-04b	Raymer	*Lavana H (Huff) Raymer*	Dec 04, 1924	Oct 15, 2004

Sect-row-plot	Surname	Given Name	Birth Date	Death Date
B-02-05	Ancestors	*Memorial to Ancestors* Buried North of Renfrow on Little Reedy Creek Golson Embry [Feb 21, 1803 - Jan 28, 1881] Mary Polly (Sublett) Embry [Nov 15, 1799 - Jan 08, 1879] William Peter Huff [1820 - Sep 28, 1848] Eveline (Embry) Huff-Embry [May 05, 1826 - Jan 28, 1867]		
B-02-08a	Woosley	*Kirby Woosley*	Aug 29, 1905	Aug 23, 1987
B-02-08b	Woosley	*Emma (Tomes) Woosley*	Sep 30, 1904	Apr 15, 1996
B-02-09a	Woosley	*Faymon D Woosley*	Mar 06, 1925	Jul 03, 1968
B-02-09b	Woosley	*Dimple (Childress) Woosley*	Sep 01, 1929	Mar 23, 2011
B-02-10a	Woosley	*Wilcy Woosley*	Jul 25, 1929	Oct 22, 2001
B-02-10b	Woosley	*Mona Laverne (Woosley) Woosley*	Oct 09, 1932	Nov 05, 2009
B-03-01 B-03-01a B-03-01b B-03-01c B-03-01d B-03-01e	Howard	*Quintuplet Infants Howard* Aden James Howard Keeley Elizabeth Howard Barrett Alexander Howard Kendall Scott Howard Zander Paul Howard	Jul 08, 2012	Jul 08, 2012
B-03-02a	Howard	*Keith Randall Howard*	Jul 19, 1983	
B-03-02b	Howard	*Whitney Elizabeth (Small) Howard*	Aug 24, 1981	
B-03-03a	Woosley	*Landon Woosley*	Jan 10, 1912	Nov 24, 2002
B-03-03b	Woosley	*Sedalia H (Huff) Woosley*	Feb 04, 1914	Apr 13, 2000
B-03-04a	Hamilton	*Andrew Graff Hamilton*	Sep 30, 1895	Apr 25, 1980
B-03-04b	Hamilton	*Pansy Mildred (Bolton) Hamilton*	Aug 23, 1902	Sep 08, 1985
B-03-05	Woosley Hamilton	Josephine wife of Major A. G. *Josephine (Hutcherson) Hamilton*	Sep 07, 1873	Mar 18, 1954
B-03-06a	Hamilton	Louis son of A.G. & Janet *Louis Millette Hamilton*	Apr 16, 1950	Apr 16, 1950
B-03-06b	Hamilton	Charles son of A.G. & Janet *Charles Henry Hamilton*	Apr 16, 1950	Apr 16, 1950
B-03-07a	Houchin	*Sim H Houchin*	Dec 18, 1922	Dec 22, 2006
B-03-07b	Houchin	*Arieta (Hamilton) Houchin*	Mar 05, 1924	Aug 26, 2014
B-04-08a	Luttrell	*Kelly Travis Luttrell*	Feb 10, 1934	Mar 12, 2007
B-04-08b	Lutrell	*Julia Ann (Woosley) Luttrell*	Feb 07, 1941	

Sect-row-plot	Surname	Given Name	Birth Date	Death Date
B-04-12a	Harrison	*William Jackson "Jack" Harrison*	Dec 14, 1930	Aug 02, 2013
B-04-12b	Harrison	*Joyce W (Woosley) Harrison*	May 12, 1931	
B-04-13a	Woosley	*Alben B Woosley*	Mar 10, 1933	
B-04-13b	Woosley	*Lillie E (Andersen) Woosley*	Jul 31, 1934	
B-04-14a	Wells	*Loyd Sherman Wells*	Jul 11, 1914	Nov 07, 1999
B-04-14b	Wells	*Urbana H (Huff) Wells*	Mar 01, 1921	Sep 06, 1992
B-04-15	Woosley	Bethany Anne dau. of Terrell & Mary Ann *Bethany Anne Woosley*	Jun 13, 1972	Jun 13, 1972
B-05-06a	Ellis	*Joseph B Ellis*	Jan 08, 1927	Jul 30, 2010
B-05-06b	Ellis	*Eurita (Davis) Ellis*	Apr 30, 1934	
B-05-07a	Tomes	*Harold Martin Tomes*	Sep 02, 1921	Aug 19, 1994
B-05-07b	Tomes	*Vida (Lindsey) Tomes*	Jan 11, 1922	
B-05-08a	Tomes	H. M. husband - married 2-22-1900 *Hammilker M "Mack" Tomes*	Mar 31, 1878	Aug 18, 1976
B-05-08b	Tomes	Ida wife *Ida E (Tomes) Tomes*	Sep 26, 1881	Jan 18, 1965
B-05-09a	Woosley	*Alton Burks Woosley*	Apr 21, 1904	Mar 01, 1994
B-05-09b	Woosley	*Edna T (Tomes) Woosley*	May 30, 1909	Nov 27, 1988
B-05-10a	Woosley	*Kendall Sheridan Woosley*	Jan 29, 1929	Apr 26, 2003
B-05-10b	Woosley	*Myra (Ellis) Woosley*	Nov 12, 1930	
B-05-11a & 11b	Lawrence	retake both sides		
B-05-11c	~~Lawrence~~ Meredith	Effie L. Meredith mother *Effie L (Lawrence) Meredith*	Dec 25, 1881	Apr 16, 1957
B-05-11d	~~Lawrence~~ Meredith	Mathie J. husband *Mathew J "Mathie" Meredith*	Oct 28, 1908	Nov 16, 1989
B-05-11e	~~Lawrence~~ Meredith	Kezzie W. wife *Kezzie (Woosley) Meredith*	Aug 31, 1909	Jan 01, 1985
B-05-12a	Woosley	George W. husband *George Washington Woosley*	Apr 25, 1869	Jan 07, 1958

Sect-row-plot	Surname	Given Name	Birth Date	Death Date
B-05-12b	Woosley	Maggie B. wife *Margaret "Maggie" (Burks) Woosley*	May 18, 1884	Apr 02, 1952
B-05-13a	Huff	Cleve husband *Thomas Cleveland "Cleve" Huff*	Jan 29, 1885	Dec 01, 1958
B-05-13b	Huff	Tina wife *Tina (Woosley) Huff*	Apr 08, 1896	Apr 19, 1988
B-06-08a	Newkirk	*James H Newkirk*	Nov 15, 1948	Feb 07, 1999
B-06-08b	Newkirk	*Jewell D (Davis) Newkirk*	Mar 16, 1949	
B-06-09	Woosley	Jimmie C. *Jimmie Coleman Woosley*	Nov 09, 1948	Nov 17, 1948
B-06-10a	Woosley	*Champion W "Champ" Woosley*	May 07, 1912	Oct 18, 1993
B-06-10b	Woosley	*Christine C (Coleman) Woosley*	Feb 22, 1911	Oct 21, 1981
B-06-11	unknown	C.W.W. reserved grave plot		
B-06-12	unknown	D.R.D. reserved grave plot		
B-06-13	unknown	S.C.D. reserved grave plot		
B-06-14	Hampton	Mary E. *Mary Elizabeth (Woosley) Hampton*	Nov 06, 1887	Jan 01, 1978
B-06-15a	Woosley	Lewis W. *Lewis Washington Woosley*	Mar 30, 1894	Feb 17, 1963
B-06-15b	Woosley	Jannie L. *Jane L "Jannie" (Woosley) Woosley*	Aug 29, 1902	Aug 20, 1975
B-07-08a	Miller	*Pansy A (unknown) Miller*	Jun 14, 1919	Aug 11, 2003
B-07-08b	Miller	*Willard C Miller*	Jun 26, 1920	Jul 15, 2006
B-07-09a	England	*James D England*	Jun 05, 1929	Dec 24, 2003
B-07-09b	England	*Alta Elizabeth "Lizzie" (Miller) England*	Mar 31, 1926	Mar 28, 2005
B-07-10	Johnson	*Pirtle Junior Johnson*	Feb 26, 1941	Mar 26, 1996
B-07-11a	Oller	S. M. *Silas Merril Oller*	Nov 23, 1873	Mar 23, 1954
B-07-11b	Oller	Anthie *Antha V "Anthie" (Elmore) Oller*	Sep 02, 1876	~~Nov 29, 1973~~ Sep 04, 1957
B-07-12a	Burkhead	Ray *Ray L Burkhead*	Dec 03, 1889	May 23, 1958
B-07-12b	Burkhead	Mary *Mary Abney (Lacefield) Burkhead*		

2 - ALPHABETICAL INDEX

Page	Sect/Row/Plot	Dates	Surname	Full Name
37	B-02-05	[N/A-N/A]	Ancestors, Memorial to	Memorial to Ancestors
32	A-23-29	[1832-1897]	Anderson, Arthur B	Arthur B Anderson
32	A-23-27	[1841-unknown]	Anderson, Charles C	Charles C Anderson
32	A-23-24	[1865-1865]	Anderson, Dartha (1860)	Dartha (1860) Anderson
10	A-06-04	[1909-1909]	Anderson, Ettie	Ettie Anderson
32	A-23-23	[1859-1859]	Anderson, Infant Daughter	Infant Daughter Anderson
32	A-23-21	[1829-1918]	Anderson, Lewis Andrew	Lewis Andrew Anderson
24	A-16-37	[unknown-unknown]	Anderson, Mary A	Mary A Anderson
32	A-23-22	[1835-1877]	Anderson, Mary Permelia	Mary Permelia (Nash) Anderson
10	A-06-02	[1879-1938]	Anderson, Senorah Roseline	Senorah Roseline (Tomes) Anderson
10	A-06-05	[1876-1918]	Anderson, Thelma Josephine	Thelma Josephine (Tomes) Anderson
32	A-23-32	[1830-1876]	Anderson, Valentine	Valentine Anderson
25	A-18-15.01	[1863-1934]	Anderson, Warren Elias	Warren Elias Anderson
31	A-22-42a	[1918-2008]	Basham, Campbell Olis	Campbell Olis Basham
31	A-22-42b	[1917-2001]	Basham, Nova	Nova (Woosley) Basham
3	A-02-08	[1907-1907]	Bolton, Avra E	Avra E Bolton
33	A-24-26	[1856-1880]	Bolton, Beverly L	Beverly L Bolton
33	A-24-25	[1815-1883]	Bolton, Dinah	Dinah (Woosley) Bolton
4	A-02-09	[1897-1900]	Bolton, Eddie B	Eddie B Bolton
3	A-02-07a	[1863-1931]	Bolton, George Morgan	George Morgan Bolton
7	A-04-02b	[1893-1976]	Bolton, George W	George W Bolton
27	A-18-25	[1845-1917]	Bolton, George Washington	George Washington Bolton
33	A-24-24	[1813-1889]	Bolton, Haile Hail	Haile Hail Bolton
33	A-24-27	[1843-1858]	Bolton, James M	James M Bolton
25	A-18-15.02	[1800-1891]	Bolton, John Riley	John Riley Bolton
33	A-24-27a	[1850-1857]	Bolton, John Riley	John Riley Bolton
33	A-24-23	[1840-1862]	Bolton, Josiah	Josiah Bolton
33	A-24-28	[1848-1855]	Bolton, Julyan	Julyan Bolton
7	A-04-02a	[1895-1975]	Bolton, Leon Stanley	Leon Stanley (Johnson) Bolton
34	A-24-36	[1837-1915]	Bolton, Lewis Franklin	Lewis Franklin Bolton
34	A-24-37	[1847-1921]	Bolton, Mary Virginia	Mary Virginia (Thacker) Bolton
2	A-01-01	[1924-1924]	Bolton, Ralph Morgan	Ralph Morgan Bolton
27	A-18-24	[1847-1878]	Bolton, Rebecca	Rebecca (Nash) Bolton
34	A-24-35b	[1853-1931]	Bolton, Samuel Haile	Samuel Haile Bolton
3	A-02-07b	[1865-1945]	Bolton, Sarah Adaline	Sarah Adaline (Lawrence) Bolton
34	A-24-35a	[1860-1930]	Bolton, Sarah Ann	Sarah Ann (Foreman) Bolton
33	A-24-34	[1881-1886]	Bolton, Valentine	Valentine Bolton
7	A-04-06	[1911-1935]	Bratcher, Clydus	Clydus Bratcher
31	A-21-41a	[1883-1976]	Bryant, John B	John B Bryant
31	A-21-41b	[1886-1974]	Bryant, Mollie	Mollie (Huff) Bryant
39	B-07-12b	[1891-]	Burkhead, Mary Abney	Mary Abney (Lacefield) Burkhead
39	B-07-12a	[1889-1958]	Burkhead, Ray L	Ray L Burkhead
25	A-18-15.04	[1928-1947]	Carwile, Nancy Catherine	Nancy Catherine Carwile
2	A-01-02a	[1891-1975]	Childress, Ella	Ella (Huff) Childress
2	A-01-02b	[1889-1967]	Childress, Hubert F	Hubert F Childress
21	A-13-18	[1873-1874]	Conway, Asa Thomas	Asa Thomas Conway
21	A-13-17	[1849-1882]	Conway, Evaline	Evaline (Willis) Conway
21	A-13-15	[1884-1884]	Conway, Lucian P	Lucian P Conway
14	A-08-05a	[1889-1926]	Cummings, Andrew Casner	Andrew Casner Cummings
14	A-08-05b	[1891-1974]	Cummings, Cora C	Cora C (Toms) Cummings
12	A-07-15	[1896-1896]	Cummings, Edward	Edward Cummings
14	A-08-05c	[1918-1926]	Cummings, Gorden	Gorden Cummings
29	A-20-36	[1844-1867]	Cummings, Rutha B	Rutha B Cummings
29	A-20-35	[1835-1865]	Cummings, Squire D	Squire D Cummings
12	A-07-13	[1855-1892]	Cummins, Elizabeth Jane	Elizabeth Jane (Woosley) Cummins
12	A-07-14	[1855-1877]	Cummins, William A	William A Cummins
19	A-12-05a	[1913-1993]	Davis, Bytha Woosley	Bytha Woosley (Hampton) Davis
19	A-12-08b	[1873-1956]	Davis, Eliza	Eliza (Woosley) Davis
19	A-12-07	[1902-1905]	Davis, Hattie Ree	Hattie Ree Davis
19	A-12-05b	[1907-1979]	Davis, Hillard	Hillard Davis
19	A-12-06	[1935-1935]	Davis, James Lewis	James Lewis Davis
19	A-12-08a	[1858-1935]	Davis, Thomas Jefferson	Thomas Jefferson Davis
3	A-02-06	[1814-1905]	Decker, Pheaba	Pheaba Decker
10	A-06-01	[1922-1922]	Decker, Samuel Allen	Samuel Allen Decker
25	A-18-15.03	[1835-1925]	Dotson, Barbara	Barbara (Miller) Dotson

24	A-16-30	[1822-1895]	Dotson, James C	James C Dotson
24	A-16-29	[1818-1866]	Dotson, Vasta Vastie	Vasta Vastie (Blakely) Dotson
9	A-05-04	[1922-1923]	Duvall, Amos	Amos Duvall
9	A-05-05	[1908-1922]	Duvall, Augustus	Augustus Duvall
9	A-05-07	[1882-1923]	Duvall, Henry Warren	Henry Warren Duvall
9	A-05-06	[1884-1923]	Duvall, Sarah Angeline Lina	Sarah Angeline Lina (Farris) Duvall
38	B-05-06b	[1934-]	Ellis, Eurita	Eurita (Davis) Ellis
38	B-05-06a	[1927-2010]	Ellis, Joseph B	Joseph B Ellis
32	A-23-34a	[1882-1965]	Embry, Callie	Callie (Ellis) Embry
32	A-23-33	[1908-1908]	Embry, Clarence	Clarence Embry
6	A-03-24	[1866-1923]	Embry, Commodore Perry	Commodore Perry Embry
6	A-03-25	[1866-1923]	Embry, Dina E	Dina E (Woosley) Embry
32	A-23-34b	[1876-1941]	Embry, Vergil Crit	Vergil Crit Embry
39	B-07-09b	[1926-2005]	England, Alta Elizabeth	Alta Elizabeth (Miller) England
39	B-07-09a	[1929-2003]	England, James D	James D England
10	A-06-15	[1877-1893]	Forman, Marrie E	Marrie E Forman
17	A-09-14	[1870-1872]	Forman, Pardine	Pardine Forman
17	A-09-13	[1876-1878]	Forman, Sarah Jane	Sarah Jane Forman
30	A-21-38a	[1892-1968]	Geary, Azro	Azro Geary
30	A-21-37	[1912-1914]	Geary, Daniel	Daniel Geary
30	A-21-38b	[1873-1937]	Geary, Perlina Lina	Perlina Lina (Willis) Geary
16	A-08-27	[1893-1952]	Goff, Dona M	Dona M Goff
6	A-03-20	[1885-1939]	Goodwin, Lula	Lula (Nash) Goodwin
12	A-06-28b	[1822-1904]	Gross, Edward	Edward Gross
12	A-06-28a	[1903-1941]	Gross, Elsie Mae	Elsie Mae (Huff) Gross
37	B-03-04a	[1895-1980]	Hamilton, Andrew Graff	Andrew Graff Hamilton
37	B-03-06b	[1950-1950]	Hamilton, Charles Henry	Charles Henry Hamilton
37	B-03-05	[1873-1954]	Hamilton, Josephine	Josephine (Hutcherson) Hamilton
37	B-03-06a	[1950-1950]	Hamilton, Louis Millette	Louis Millette Hamilton
37	B-03-04b	[1902-1985]	Hamilton, Pansy Mildred	Pansy Mildred (Bolton) Hamilton
39	B-06-14	[1887-1978]	Hampton, Mary Elizabeth	Mary Elizabeth (Woosley) Hampton
3	A-01-15	[1897-1899]	Hardin, Charles Wesley	Charles Wesley Hardin
18	A-10-35	[1890-1890]	Hardin, D Gilbert	D Gilbert Hardin
18	A-10-36	[1861-1890]	Hardin, Nancy Catherine	Nancy Catherine (Tomes) Hardin
38	B-04-12b	[1931-]	Harrison, Joyce	Joyce (Woosley) Harrison
38	B-04-12a	[1930-2013]	Harrison, William Jackson	William Jackson Harrison
21	A-14-24	[1910-1910]	Hayes, Hurshal T	Hurshal T Hayes
37	B-03-07b	[1924-2014]	Houchin, Arieta	Arieta (Hamilton) Houchin
37	B-03-07a	[1922-2006]	Houchin, Sim H	Sim H Houchin
37	B-03-01a	[2012-2012]	Howard, Arden James	Arden James Howard
37	B-03-01c	[2012-2012]	Howard, Barrett Alexander	Barrett Alexander Howard
37	B-03-01b	[2012-2012]	Howard, Keely Elizabeth	Keely Elizabeth Howard
37	B-03-02a	[1983-]	Howard, Keith Randall	Keith Randall Howard
37	B-03-01d	[2012-2012]	Howard, Kendall Scott	Kendall Scott Howard
37	B-03-01	[2012-2012]	Howard, Quintuplet Infants	Quintuplet Infants Howard
37	B-03-02b	[1981-]	Howard, Whitney Elizabeth	Whitney Elizabeth (Small) Howard
37	B-03-01e	[2012-2012]	Howard, Zander Paul	Zander Paul Howard
8	A-04-11	[1879-1895]	Huff, Alfred	Alfred Huff
12	A-07-17a	[1857-1919]	Huff, Alfred	Alfred Huff
8	A-04-10a	[1852-1938]	Huff, Allen	Allen Huff
14	A-08-08	[1897-1930]	Huff, Alta	Alta (Lee) Huff
36	B-01-02b	[1891-1970]	Huff, Anthia Gerter	Anthia Gerter (Huff) Huff
15	A-08-20b	[1862-1941]	Huff, Bedford	Bedford Huff
36	B-01-04b	[1895-1984]	Huff, Blanche Rebecca	Blanche Rebecca (Huff) Huff
17	A-09-20	[1824-1901]	Huff, Catherine	Catherine (Lee) Huff
2	A-01-04a	[1889-1973]	Huff, Chester	Chester Huff
36	B-01-04a	[1889-1973]	Huff, Chester	Chester Huff
11	A-06-27a	[1881-1955]	Huff, Commodore Perry	Commodore Perry Huff
36	B-01-03a	[1924-2009]	Huff, Denby	Denby Huff
7	A-04-09a	[1880-1940]	Huff, Dina Elizabeth	Dina Elizabeth (Nash) Huff
13	A-07-29	[1874-1964]	Huff, Elizabeth Lizzie	Elizabeth Lizzie (Woosley) Huff
2	A-01-03a	[1897-1994]	Huff, Elmer E Jane	Elmer E Jane (Embry) Huff
7	A-04-07a	[1894-1927]	Huff, George W	George W Huff
8	A-04-09b	[1881-1973]	Huff, George Washington	George Washington Huff
36	B-01-06	[1922-2012]	Huff, Gertrude	Gertrude (Whoberry) Huff
2	A-01-03b	[1889-1983]	Huff, Gilbert Elbert	Gilbert Elbert Huff

10	A-06-16	[1901-1901]	Huff, Graften	Graften Huff
36	B-01-03b	[1920-1927]	Huff, Hazel Dawn	Hazel Dawn (Clark) Huff
36	B-01-01a	[1897-1988]	Huff, Herbert	Herbert Huff
5	A-03-08	[1911-1911]	Huff, Ida Gertrude	Ida Gertrude Huff
29	A-21-18	[1871-1873]	Huff, James	James Huff
13	A-07-17b	[1860-1947]	Huff, Julia Ann	Julia Ann (Woosley) Huff
15	A-08-22	[1881-1882]	Huff, Laura Bell	Laura Bell Huff
13	A-07-30	[1872-1917]	Huff, Leonard Peter	Leonard Peter Huff
26	A-18-15F	[1781-1851]	Huff, Leonard Peter	Leonard Peter Huff
7	A-04-07b	[1901-]	Huff, Leva	Leva (unknown) Huff
36	B-01-05	[1947-]	Huff, Madolyn C	Madolyn C () Huff
28	A-20-12a	[1844-1912]	Huff, Martha Jane	Martha Jane (Woosley) Huff
11	A-06-17b	[1865-1937]	Huff, Marvel A	Marvel A Huff
16	A-08-29a	[1871-1943]	Huff, Mary Ann	Mary Ann (Willis) Huff
28	A-20-11	[1888-1920]	Huff, Matchless	Matchless Huff
26	A-18-15b	[1783-1852]	Huff, Nancy B	Nancy B (Pharis) Huff
11	A-06-17a	[1869-1929]	Huff, Nancy Candus	Nancy Candus (Miller) Huff
17	A-09-21	[1816-1878]	Huff, Nathan	Nathan Huff
11	A-06-27b	[1884-1949]	Huff, Nellie Lucy	Nellie Lucy (Jones) Huff
23	A-16-14	[1893-1895]	Huff, Owens	Owens Huff
17	A-09-19	[1865-1920]	Huff, Paradine	Paradine Huff
29	A-21-19	[1862-1864]	Huff, Pendleton	Pendleton Huff
15	A-08-20a	[1864-1908]	Huff, Priscilla Jane	Priscilla Jane (Bryant) Huff
8	A-04-10b	[1855-1944]	Huff, Rebecca	Rebecca (Woosley) Huff
2	A-01-04a	[1869-1928]	Huff, Rebecca Belle	Rebecca Belle (Woosley) Huff
36	B-01-02a	[1891-1961]	Huff, Roscoe	Roscoe Huff
29	A-21-17	[1872-1884]	Huff, Sarah E	Sarah E Huff
28	A-20-12b	[1847-1890]	Huff, Sidney	Sidney Huff
16	A-08-29b	[1871-1956]	Huff, Sidney A	Sidney A Huff
28	A-20-13	[1875-1876]	Huff, Simeon G	Simeon G Huff
2	A-01-04b	[1859-1945]	Huff, Stanford	Stanford Huff
2	A-01-01b	[1898-1979]	Huff, Stella Setta	Stella Setta (Tomes) Huff
7	A-04-03	[1842-1921]	Huff, Susanna Leudena	Susanna Leudena (Nash) Huff
39	B-05-13a	[1885-1958]	Huff, Thomas Cleveland	Thomas Cleveland Huff
39	B-05-13b	[1896-1988]	Huff, Tina	Tina (Woosley) Huff
7	A-04-04	[1842-1908]	Huff, William	William Huff
8	A-04-12	[1877-1955]	Huff, William Albert	William Albert Huff
26	A-18-20	[1858-1885]	Hunt, Eliza	Eliza (Nash) Hunt
26	A-18-16	[1811-1876]	Hunt, Gemima	Gemima (Wommack) Hunt
33	A-24-32	[1868-1890]	Hunt, George	George Hunt
33	A-24-33	[1838-1881]	Hunt, George W	George W Hunt
33	A-24-30	[1863-1863]	Hunt, Julia Ann	Julia Ann Hunt
26	A-18-17	[1805-1878]	Hunt, Willis	Willis Hunt
3	A-02-02	[1909-1975]	Johnson, Ersa	Ersa (Miller) Johnson
39	B-07-10	[1941-1996]	Johnson, Pirtle Junior	Pirtle Junior Johnson
25	A-18-04	[1912-2005]	Johnson, Sally Frances	Sally Frances (Miller) Johnson
12	A-07-11	[1882-1882]	Jones, Infant Son	Infant Son Jones
29	A-20-40	[1846-1920]	Jones, Jacob D	Jacob D Jones
12	A-07-10	[1879-1881]	Jones, James Albert	James Albert Jones
12	A-07-12b	[1861-1939]	Jones, John Crittenden	John Crittenden Jones
12	A-07-12a	[1862-1947]	Jones, Loueller	Loueller (Woosley) Jones
30	A-21-28	[1846-1880]	Jones, Manerva	Manerva (Willis) Jones
28	A-20-26	[unknown-unknown]	Jones, Mary	Mary (unknown) Jones
30	A-21-27	[1867-1868]	Jones, Nancy Elizabeth	Nancy Elizabeth Jones
28	A-20-25	[1834-1858]	Jones, Thomas	Thomas Jones
6	A-03-23b	[1952-2014]	Lashley, Charles A	Charles A Lashley
6	A-03-23a	[1947-]	Lashley, Texie Sue	Texie Sue (Torrence) Lashley
38	B-05-11a & b	[-]	Lawrence,	Lawrence
35	A-26-29	[1795-1869]	Lee, Barnett	Barnett Lee
35	A-26-30	[1800-1881]	Lee, Sarah	Sarah (Parrot) Lee
34	A-26-26	[1866-1868]	Lee, Viola Y	Viola Y Lee
26	A-18-15a	[1834-1852]	Lee, William	William Lee
34	A-26-28	[1834-1852]	Lee, William	William Lee
7	A-04-01a	[1933-1935]	Lindsey, Cuba Darwin	Cuba Darwin Lindsey
7	A-04-01b	[1914-1929]	Lindsey, Marjorie	Marjorie Lindsey
37	B-04-08b	[1941-]	Luttrell, Julia Ann	Julia Ann (Woosley) Luttrell

37	B-04-08a	[1934-2007]	Luttrell, Kelly Travis	Kelly Travis Luttrell
34	A-24-38	[1915-2005]	Mattingly, James Gordon	James Gordon Mattingly
38	B-05-11c	[1881-1957]	Meredith, Effie L	Effie L (Lawrence) Meredith
38	B-05-11e	[1909-1985]	Meredith, Kezzie W	Kezzie W (Woosley) Meredith
38	B-05-11d	[1908-1989]	Meredith, Mathew J	Mathew J Meredith
33	A-24-20	[1801-1888]	Miller, Abraham Kingery	Abraham Kingery Miller
18	A-09-26	[1897-1899]	Miller, Ada B	Ada B Miller
17	A-09-25	[1880-1880]	Miller, Alice D	Alice D Miller
17	A-09-24	[1851-1880]	Miller, Alice J	Alice J (Hardin) Miller
34	A-26-19a	[1869-1870]	Miller, Argalas	Argalas Miller
15	A-08-18b	[1838-1926]	Miller, Artemecia Artie Michie	Artemecia Artie Michie (Tomes) Miller
15	A-08-18a	[1832-1926]	Miller, Arthur Beau Nash	Arthur Beau Nash Miller
19	A-12-01	[1930-1943]	Miller, Arvin V	Arvin V Miller
13	A-07-25b	[1881-1929]	Miller, Bertha	Bertha (Woosley) Miller
12	A-07-04	[1899-1911]	Miller, Caladonia	Caladonia (Cummings) Miller
20	A-12-19	[1801-1858]	Miller, Christopher	Christopher Miller
31	A-23-18	[1801-1858]	Miller, Christopher	Christopher Miller
32	A-23-20	[1844-1870]	Miller, Christopher C	Christopher C Miller
5	A-03-11	[1885-1957]	Miller, Cornelius	Cornelius Miller
3	A-02-04	[1929-1929]	Miller, Earleen	Earleen Miller
34	A-26-18	[1870-1871]	Miller, Eleanor	Eleanor Miller
15	A-08-19	[1864-1927]	Miller, Elizabeth	Elizabeth Miller
19	A-12-04a	[1899-1987]	Miller, Frances	Frances (Lashley) Miller
20	A-12-22	[1870-1870]	Miller, Infant Daughter	Infant Daughter Miller
20	A-12-23	[1825-1903]	Miller, John Meredith	John Meredith Miller
4	A-02-12	[1854-1922]	Miller, Laura Ann	Laura Ann (Basham) Miller
4	A-02-16	[1863-1895]	Miller, Lewis Morgan	Lewis Morgan Miller
16	A-09-01a	[1907-1980]	Miller, Lillie Mable	Lillie Mable (Hunt) Miller
16	A-09-01b	[1905-1971]	Miller, Lloyd Wesley	Lloyd Wesley Miller
14	A-07-35a	[1937-]	Miller, Lois A	Lois A (unknown) Miller
3	A-02-03a	[1879-1968]	Miller, Margaret T	Margaret T (Basham) Miller
5	A-03-09	[1894-1895]	Miller, Martha E	Martha E Miller
5	A-03-10	[1875-1895]	Miller, Mary J	Mary J (Jones) Miller
3	A-02-05	[1901-1905]	Miller, Mary Lavelle	Mary Lavelle Miller
19	A-12-02	[1932-1943]	Miller, Mary M	Mary M Miller
4	A-02-15a	[1830-1915]	Miller, Melissa A	Melissa A (Woosley) Miller
31	A-23-17	[1805-1868]	Miller, Nancy Hundley	Nancy Hundley (Nash) Miller
25	A-18-15.05	[1805-1868]	Miller, Ova B	Ova B Miller
19	A-12-04b	[1895-1970]	Miller, Ova Vesterfield	Ova Vesterfield Miller
13	A-07-25a	[1880-1964]	Miller, Palmon C	Palmon C Miller
39	B-07-08a	[1919-2003]	Miller, Pansy A	Pansy A (unknown) Miller
17	A-09-23	[1857-1937]	Miller, Pinkney	Pinkney Miller
33	A-24-19	[1808-1883]	Miller, Rachel	Rachel (Musick) Miller
6	A-03-17	[1875-1961]	Miller, Rebecca	Rebecca Miller
20	A-12-24	[1831-1873]	Miller, Rebecca	Rebecca (Woosley) Miller
19	A-12-03	[1935-1935]	Miller, Roy William	Roy William Miller
4	A-02-15b	[1826-1916]	Miller, Samuel	Samuel Miller
20	A-12-25	[1854-1870]	Miller, Samuel M	Samuel M Miller
26	A-18-15.06	[1944-1945]	Miller, Sandra Pearl	Sandra Pearl Miller
34	A-26-19b	[1869-1870]	Miller, Silvanus S	Silvanus S Miller
16	A-08-33	[1896-1935]	Miller, Walter Edward	Walter Edward Miller
3	A-02-03b	[1874-1944]	Miller, Wesley Davis	Wesley Davis Miller
39	B-07-08b	[1920-2006]	Miller, Willard C	Willard C Miller
14	A-07-35b	[1933-1996]	Miller, William D	William D Miller
20	A-12-26	[1850-1850]	Miller, William H	William H Miller
21	A-15-02	[1908-1953]	Minton, Helen P	Helen P (Tomes) Minton
29	A-20-33	[1862-1864]	Minton, Ollevi	Ollevi Minton
36	B-02-03b	[1905-1991]	Morse, Delphia W	Delphia W (Woosley) Morse
36	B-02-03a	[1904-1982]	Morse, Ownard D	Ownard D Morse
23	A-16-23	[1814-1889]	Nash, Anderson Allan	Anderson Allan Nash
23	A-16-24	[1844-1866]	Nash, Arthur Beau	Arthur Beau Nash
28	A-20-24	[1818-1862]	Nash, Arthur Beau	Arthur Beau Nash
30	A-21-21	[1780-1854]	Nash, Arthur Beau	Arthur Beau Nash
22	A-15-09	[1855-1933]	Nash, Buford Walker	Buford Walker Nash
27	A-18-22	[1810-1864]	Nash, Buford Walker	Buford Walker Nash
13	A-07-21	[1884-1886]	Nash, Burtes	Burtes Nash

18	A-11-42	[1891-1931]	Nash, Charles F	Charles F Nash
24	A-16-42b	[1844-1932]	Nash, Daniel	Daniel Nash
23	A-16-16	[1841-1908]	Nash, Demarcus Lafayette	Demarcus Lafayette Nash
22	A-15-10	[1885-1904]	Nash, Edmon Ellwood	Edmon Ellwood Nash
10	A-05-14	[1863-1931]	Nash, Elijah A	Elijah A Nash
27	A-18-21	[1820-1924]	Nash, Elizabeth Betsey	Elizabeth Betsey (Woosley) Nash
13	A-07-19	[1856-1932]	Nash, Elvira Jane	Elvira Jane (Woosley) Nash
9	A-05-08	[1847-1927]	Nash, Emma	Emma (Williams) Nash
22	A-15-08	[1847-1927]	Nash, Emma	Emma (Williams) Nash
23	A-16-25	[-]	Nash, Emory	Emory Nash
18	A-11-39	[1904-1923]	Nash, Eva Evie	Eva Evie Nash
27	A-18-23	[1853-1872]	Nash, George Clinton	George Clinton Nash
18	A-11-41	[1867-1939]	Nash, Hardie	Hardie Nash
10	A-05-19	[1886-1886]	Nash, Herbit	Herbit Nash
15	A-08-21	[1900-1900]	Nash, Infant Daughter	Infant Daughter Nash
22	A-15-11	[1888-1888]	Nash, Infant Daughter	Infant Daughter Nash
18	A-09-30	[1904-1904]	Nash, Infant Twin Sons	Infant Twin Sons Nash
31	A-22-16	[1841-1878]	Nash, James B Warren	James B Warren Nash
23	A-16-19	[1868-1880]	Nash, James Pendleton	James Pendleton Nash
3	A-02-01	[1928-1929]	Nash, Jeanetta Lucille	Jeanetta Lucille Nash
16	A-08-34	[1897-1973]	Nash, Jesse James	Jesse James Nash
6	A-03-21	[1857-1934]	Nash, John H	John H Nash
18	A-11-40	[1873-1930]	Nash, Lola Biddie	Lola Biddie (Crowder) Nash
23	A-16-17	[1846-1886]	Nash, Louisiana Lousey	Louisiana Lousey (Phelps) Nash
24	A-16-42a	[1847-1918]	Nash, Lucrecia	Lucrecia (Willis) Nash
10	A-05-15	[1868-1919]	Nash, Lucy Ann	Lucy Ann (Goodwin) Nash
6	A-03-22	[1858-1903]	Nash, Margaret	Margaret (Foreman) Nash
23	A-16-22	[1815-1878]	Nash, Margaret Peggy	Margaret Peggy (Baker) Nash
25	A-18-12	[1846-1873]	Nash, Marvel	Marvel Nash
23	A-16-21	[1870-1880]	Nash, Mary M	Mary M Nash
31	A-22-23	[1824-1855]	Nash, Mary Polly	Mary Polly (Willis) Nash
13	A-07-18a	[1878-1945]	Nash, Millard	Millard Nash
29	A-21-20	[1784-1859]	Nash, Milly	Milly (Toms) Nash
31	A-22-21	[1834-1877]	Nash, Nancy Hundley	Nancy Hundley (Miller) Nash
13	A-07-18b	[1880-1930]	Nash, Oma Wise	Oma Wise (Huff) Nash
13	A-07-20	[1852-1918]	Nash, Samuel M	Samuel M Nash
10	A-05-18	[1877-1877]	Nash, Thomas	Thomas Nash
34	A-26-20	[1850-]	Nash, Thurv	Thurv Nash
23	A-16-18	[1965-1886]	Nash, William Thomas	William Thomas Nash
31	A-22-22	[1863-1864]	Nash, William Warren	William Warren Nash
9	A-05-01	[1890-1937]	Nash-Lewsader, Irene	Irene (Huff) Nash-Lewsader
26	A-18-15g	[-]	Negro Slave, Aunt Lottie	Aunt Lottie Negro Slave
39	B-06-08a	[1948-1999]	Newkirk, James H	James H Newkirk
39	B-06-08b	[1949-]	Newkirk, Jewell D	Jewell D (Davis) Newkirk
27	A-18-36	[1881-1899]	Oller, A Lenia	A Lenia Oller
39	B-07-11b	[1876-1973]	Oller, Anthe V Anthie	Anthe V Anthie (Elmore) Oller
26	A-18-15.07	[1800-1849]	Oller, Cynthia F	Cynthia F (Hunt) Oller
2	A-01-08	[1867-1941]	Oller, Cynthia Francis	Cynthia Francis Oller
6	A-03-18	[1866-1917]	Oller, Eliza Lide	Eliza Lide (Miller) Oller
20	A-12-15	[1867-1875]	Oller, George Washington	George Washington Oller
8	A-04-19	[1896-1896]	Oller, Gladys	Gladys Oller
31	A-22-25	[1829-1854]	Oller, Holy Matchless	Holy Matchless Oller
20	A-12-14	[1799-1875]	Oller, James B	James B Oller
6	A-03-14	[1837-1915]	Oller, James Marshall	James Marshall Oller
6	A-03-19	[1865-1947]	Oller, James Marshall Matchless	James Marshall Matchless Oller
6	A-03-12b	[1870-1923]	Oller, Joseph Terrell	Joseph Terrell Oller
8	A-04-15	[1869-1939]	Oller, Julia Ann	Julia Ann Oller
8	A-04-18	[1885-1890]	Oller, Lewis F	Lewis F Oller
5	A-03-12a	[1874-]	Oller, Martha Ellen	Martha Ellen (unknown) Oller
6	A-03-13	[1845-1917]	Oller, Mary Jane	Mary Jane (Woosley) Oller
8	A-04-17	[1883-1885]	Oller, Morris	Morris Oller
8	A-04-16b	[1856-1905]	Oller, Rachael Adeline	Rachael Adeline (Nash) Oller
39	B-07-11a	[1873-1954]	Oller, Silas Merril	Silas Merril Oller
8	A-04-16a	[1859-1931]	Oller, Thomas MacEntire	Thomas MacEntire Oller
31	A-22-24	[1832-1863]	Oller-Willis, Lucinda	Lucinda (Johnson) Oller-Willis
13	A-07-31	[1937-2002]	Pawley, Jo Ann	Jo Ann (unknown) Pawley

30	A-21-36	[1872-1893]	Preston, Margaret E	Margaret E (Willis) Preston
36	B-02-04a	[1924-1983]	Raymer, Berthel	Berthel Raymer
16	A-08-26	[1863-1896]	Raymer, Bub	Bub Raymer
23	A-16-07b	[1901-1979]	Raymer, Charles Estil	Charles Estil Raymer
23	A-16-28	[1910-1911]	Raymer, Clara C	Clara C Raymer
22	A-16-06	[1924-1926]	Raymer, J Pauline	J Pauline Raymer
36	B-02-04b	[1924-2004]	Raymer, Lavana H	Lavana H Raymer
22	A-16-07a	[1902-1981]	Raymer, Trulia	Trulia (Tomes) Raymer
35	A-28-40	[1895-1969]	Reddish, Mittie Crysal	Mittie Crysal (Hultz) Reddish
5	A-03-04	[1930-1931]	Seaton, Ermal Marie Rene	Ermal Marie Rene Seaton
5	A-03-05	[1927-1929]	Seaton, Estel Guthery	Estel Guthery Seaton
5	A-03-06	[1902-1931]	Seaton, Roy Estill	Roy Estill Seaton
35	A-27-22	[1869-1885]	Simpson, Adaline	Adaline Simpson
35	A-27-23	[1867-1944]	Simpson, Addieville	Addieville Simpson
35	A-27-20	[1787-1863]	Simpson, Azel	Azel Simpson
35	A-29-30	[1850-]	Simpson, Henry	Henry Simpson
26	A-18-15.09	[1814-1859]	Simpson, Henry Lynn	Henry Lynn Simpson
34	A-25-33	[1823-unknown]	Simpson, James	James Simpson
34	A-25-34	[1868-1879]	Simpson, James E	James E Simpson
26	A-18-15.08	[1841-1872]	Simpson, James Ward	James Ward Simpson
26	A-18-15.10	[1858-1879]	Simpson, Jesse S	Jesse S Simpson
35	A-27-21b	[1844-1869]	Simpson, John E	John E Simpson
26	A-18-15d	[1853-1861]	Simpson, Marion	Marion Simpson
35	A-27-21a	[1845-1911]	Simpson, Martha E	Martha E (Huff) Simpson
35	A-29-31	[1853-1861]	Simpson, Marton=Marion	Marton=Marion Simpson
20	A-13-01	[1937-1937]	Smith, Helen L	Helen L Smith
36	B-02-02b	[1950-2012]	Smith, Joann	Joann (Woosley) Smith
36	B-02-02a	[1948-]	Smith, Larry	Larry Smith
29	A-20-44	[1905-1983]	Swift, Victoria	Victoria (Embry) Swift
35	A-28-39	[1945-1993]	Tapscott, Delphia Lucille	Delphia Lucille (Lindsey) Tapscott
22	A-15-04	[1877-1945]	Tomes, Alvy	Alvy Tomes
14	A-08-09	[1848-1931]	Tomes, Anderson A	Anderson A Tomes
10	A-05-11	[1860-1916]	Tomes, Andrew G	Andrew G Tomes
24	A-16-38	[1920-1920]	Tomes, Clara	Clara Tomes
2	A-01-12a	[1877-1951]	Tomes, Clarissa Cathern	Clarissa Cathern (Woosley) Tomes
3	A-01-12b	[1875-1959]	Tomes, Commodore Perry	Commodore Perry Tomes
4	A-02-11a	[1861-1946]	Tomes, Cynthia Ann	Cynthia Ann (Miller) Tomes
25	A-18-01a	[1915-2014]	Tomes, Dora G	Dora G (Geary) Tomes
21	A-15-01a	[1919-1970]	Tomes, Dorothy L	Dorothy L (Huff) Tomes
20	A-13-07b	[1946-1998]	Tomes, Dwight Travis	Dwight Travis Tomes
25	A-18-02a	[1931-1931]	Tomes, Elaine	Elaine Tomes
16	A-09-09	[1832-1906]	Tomes, Elizabeth	Elizabeth (Tomes) Tomes
21	A-15-01b	[1917-2003]	Tomes, Emery Sherman	Emery Sherman Tomes
5	A-03-01a	[1906-1969]	Tomes, Esse Porter	Esse Porter Tomes
14	A-08-06b	[1898-1973]	Tomes, Eunice Bethel	Eunice Bethel (Toms) Tomes
38	B-05-08a	[1878-1976]	Tomes, Hammilker Mack	Hammilker Mack Tomes
23	A-16-27	[1874-1901]	Tomes, Hannibal	Hannibal Tomes
38	B-05-07a	[1921-1994]	Tomes, Harold Martin	Harold Martin Tomes
24	A-16-31	[1875-1914]	Tomes, Hasibal	Hasibal Tomes
12	A-07-01b	[1913-1980]	Tomes, Hayward Pirtle	Hayward Pirtle Tomes
2	A-01-11	[1908-1908]	Tomes, Hubert F	Hubert F Tomes
38	B-05-08b	[1881-1965]	Tomes, Ida E	Ida E (Tomes) Tomes
4	A-02-11b	[1858-1940]	Tomes, Indiman D	Indiman D Tomes
15	A-08-13	[????-????]	Tomes, Infant	Infant Tomes
23	A-16-10	[1945-1945]	Tomes, Infant Daughter	Infant Daughter Tomes
32	A-23-19	[1830-1864]	Tomes, J	J Tomes
2	A-01-07a	[1840-1922]	Tomes, James Buchanan	James Buchanan Tomes
14	A-08-02	[1944-2003]	Tomes, James Dolittle	James Dolittle Tomes
14	A-08-03	[1966-1967]	Tomes, James Dwayne	James Dwayne Tomes
22	A-15-06	[1904-1926]	Tomes, Jesse	Jesse Tomes
14	A-08-04a	[1877-1965]	Tomes, Jesse Board	Jesse Board Tomes
25	A-18-01b	[1906-1983]	Tomes, John	John Tomes
14	A-08-10	[1854-1934]	Tomes, Julia Ann	Julia Ann (Woosley) Tomes
12	A-07-02a	[1934-]	Tomes, Kelvin	Kelvin Tomes
25	A-18-02b	[1905-1931]	Tomes, Leona C	Leona C (Cummings) Tomes
20	A-13-07a	[1946-1984]	Tomes, Linda Darleen	Linda Darleen (Perry) Tomes

14	A-08-04b	[1878-1964]	Tomes, Lura D	Lura D (Phelps) Tomes
18	A-10-30	[1840-1881]	Tomes, Martha Ann	Martha Ann (Metcalf) Tomes
18	A-09-29	[1892-1892]	Tomes, Martha E	Martha E Tomes
22	A-15-05	[1879-1963]	Tomes, Nora Frances	Nora Frances (Harrell) Tomes
12	A-07-02b	[1932-]	Tomes, Ottie	Ottie (unknown) Tomes
21	A-15-03	[1910-1996]	Tomes, Pirtle D	Pirtle D Tomes
2	A-01-07b	[1850-1930]	Tomes, Rebecca	Rebecca (Miller) Tomes
12	A-07-01a	[1916-2003]	Tomes, Ruby Cecil	Ruby Cecil (Embry) Tomes
5	A-03-01b	[1913-1935]	Tomes, Stelsa M	Stelsa M (Haynes) Tomes
14	A-08-06a	[1890-1958]	Tomes, Thomas Franklin	Thomas Franklin Tomes
38	B-05-07b	[1922-]	Tomes, Vida	Vida (Lindsey) Tomes
4	A-02-10	[1884-1957]	Tomes, Wiley F	Wiley F Tomes
15	A-08-11	[1876-1879]	Tomes, Wiley F	Wiley F Tomes
2	A-01-06	[1917-1921]	Tomes, Zula Glendeen	Zula Glendeen Tomes
10	A-05-13	[1814-1896]	Toms, Bluford	Bluford Toms
18	A-10-32	[1865-1868]	Toms, Bluford	Bluford Toms
15	A-08-15	[1852-1941]	Toms, Cintha Ann	Cintha Ann (Woosley) Toms
28	A-20-18	[1856-1859]	Toms, Elias W	Elias W Toms
28	A-20-17	[1852-1852]	Toms, Infant Son	Infant Son Toms
17	A-09-11	[1850-1880]	Toms, James C	James C Toms
20	A-12-28	[1865-1867]	Toms, James R	James R Toms
15	A-08-14	[1840-1908]	Toms, Jasper Thomas	Jasper Thomas Toms
15	A-08-12	[1880-1903]	Toms, Martha Washington	Martha Washington Torns
26	A-18-15.11	[1830-1864]	Toms, Milly	Milly (Miller) Toms
32	A-23-18b	[1830-1864]	Toms, Milly	Milly (Miller) Toms
10	A-05-12	[1819-1899]	Toms, Rebecca	Rebecca (Baker) Toms
18	A-10-31	[1838-1907]	Toms, Redmon T	Redmon T Toms
17	A-09-10	[1870-1880]	Toms, S J	S J Toms
24	A-17-26	[1867-1868]	Toms, Thomas G	Thomas G Toms
25	A-18-15	[-]	Unmarked Graves, Memorial to	Memorial to Unmarked Graves
2	A-01-05a	[1864-1939]	Vincent, Calvernia Ancenia	Calvernia Ancenia (Willis) Vincent
2	A-01-05b	[1864-1948]	Vincent, Gillis F	Gillis F Vincent
5	A-03-07	[1906-2000]	Vincent, Theresa Thursa	Theresa Thursa (Miller) Vincent
22	A-16-05	[1950-1950]	Webb, Kenneth Michael	Kenneth Michael Webb
38	B-04-14a	[1914-1999]	Wells, Loyd Sherman	Loyd Sherman Wells
38	B-04-14b	[1921-1992]	Wells, Urbana H	Urbana H (Huff) Wells
14	A-07-33	[1871-1943]	Wilkins, Callie	Callie (unknown) Wilkins
14	A-07-34	[1869-1941]	Wilkins, Robert Newton	Robert Newton Wilkins
29	A-20-43a	[1923-1969]	Williams, Connard	Connard Williams
28	A-19-39b	[1917-2002]	Williams, Hargus	Hargus Williams
29	A-20-43b	[1924-1967]	Williams, Irene	Irene (Swift) Williams
31	A-21-39b	[1878-1942]	Williams, John Calvin	John Calvin Williams
22	A-15-13	[1799-1873]	Williams, John Haley	John Haley Williams
30	A-21-39a	[1884-1967]	Williams, Josephine Josie	Josephine Josie (Huff) Williams
22	A-15-12	[1808-1877]	Williams, Martha	Martha (Woosley) Williams
28	A-19-39a	[1925-1894]	Williams, Revil C	Revil C (Brooks) Williams
31	A-21-40	[1903-1973]	Williams, William Goebel	William Goebel Williams
27	A-18-30	[1825-1879]	Willis, Amanda	Amanda (Dotson) Willis
30	A-21-30	[1871-1888]	Willis, Anderson A	Anderson A Willis
27	A-18-31	[1819-1906]	Willis, Archibald	Archibald Willis
6	A-03-15	[1814-1895]	Willis, Asbery	Asbery Willis
29	A-20-31	[1861-1861]	Willis, Cader	Cader Willis
31	A-22-37	[1925-1925]	Willis, Charles Ray	Charles Ray Willis
18	A-11-35a	[1879-1950]	Willis, Cora Elizabeth	Cora Elizabeth (Ward) Willis
30	A-21-25	[1823-1882]	Willis, Daniel	Daniel Willis
18	A-11-35b	[1870-1927]	Willis, Daniel Boone	Daniel Boone Willis
27	A-18-33	[1881-1882]	Willis, Dora	Dora Willis
30	A-21-24	[1826-1882]	Willis, Elizabeth Tolbert	Elizabeth Tolbert (Miller) Willis
18	A-11-36	[1901-1926]	Willis, Floyd	Floyd Willis
29	A-20-28b	[1848-1916]	Willis, George Melvin	George Melvin Willis
25	A-17-35	[1894-1894]	Willis, Infant Daughter	Infant Daughter Willis
24	A-16-36	[1891-1891]	Willis, Infant Son	Infant Son Willis
25	A-17-36	[1887-1888]	Willis, Infant Son	Infant Son Willis
6	A-03-16	[1845-1917]	Willis, James Melvin	James Melvin Willis
21	A-13-14	[1847-]	Willis, Nancy	Nancy Willis
30	A-21-26	[1847-1863]	Willis, Nancy	Nancy Willis

17	A-09-17	[1849-1925]	Willis, Pheba F	Pheba F (Woosley) Willis
28	A-20-28a	[1849-1916]	Willis, Rebecca A	Rebecca A (Nash) Willis
8	A-04-13b	[1839-1927]	Willis, Serena	Serena (Miller) Willis
31	A-23-16	[1867-1870]	Willis, Susan California	Susan California Willis
8	A-04-13a	[1842-1925]	Willis, Volentine T	Volentine T Willis
17	A-09-16	[1845-1875]	Willis, Wiley	Wiley Willis
21	A-14-25	[1868-1890]	Wilson, Anderson W	Anderson W Wilson
21	A-14-26	[1840-1918]	Wilson, Dorothy Dolly	Dorothy Dolly (Nash) Wilson
21	A-14-27	[1834-1872]	Wilson, Thomas J	Thomas J Wilson
11	A-06-19b	[1886-1930]	Woosley, Addie V	Addie V (Huff) Woosley
38	B-04-13a	[1933-]	Woosley, Alben	Alben Woosley
22	A-15-15	[1877-1945]	Woosley, Alberta	Alberta (Miller) Woosley
38	B-05-09a	[1904-1994]	Woosley, Alton Burks	Alton Burks Woosley
16	A-09-07a	[1883-1953]	Woosley, Bedford R	Bedford R Woosley
38	B-04-15	[1972-1972]	Woosley, Bethany Anne	Bethany Anne Woosley
4	A-02-20b	[1865-1951]	Woosley, Bluford W	Bluford W Woosley
9	A-04-26	[1946-1966]	Woosley, Carol Sue	Carol Sue Woosley
39	B-06-10a	[1912-1999]	Woosley, Champion W	Champion W Woosley
39	B-06-10b	[1911-1981]	Woosley, Christine C	Christine C (Coleman) Woosley
5	A-03-02b	[1900-1973]	Woosley, Claudius Robert	Claudius Robert Woosley
22	A-15-14	[1877-1952]	Woosley, Curtis Blakely	Curtis Blakely Woosley
9	A-04-27	[1951-1966]	Woosley, Deanna Lynn	Deanna Lynn Woosley
19	A-12-09	[1885-1888]	Woosley, Della	Della Woosley
37	B-02-09b	[1929-2011]	Woosley, Dimple	Dimple (Childress) Woosley
38	B-05-09b	[1909-1988]	Woosley, Edna T	Edna T (Tomes) Woosley
11	A-06-25	[1891-1891]	Woosley, Effa	Effa Woosley
11	A-06-21	[1828-1883]	Woosley, Elizabeth	Elizabeth (Oller) Woosley
24	A-17-28	[1861-1861]	Woosley, Elizabeth J	Elizabeth J Woosley
5	A-02-22b	[1870-1951]	Woosley, Elmeda Meda	Elmeda Meda (Embrey) Woosley
37	B-02-08b	[1904-1996]	Woosley, Emma	Emma (Tomes) Woosley
36	B-01-07a	[1963-]	Woosley, Eric Richard	Eric Richard Woosley
20	A-13-08	[1891-1911]	Woosley, Eva	Eva (Durbin) Woosley
37	B-02-09a	[1925-1968]	Woosley, Faymon D	Faymon D Woosley
36	B-02-01b	[1924-1987]	Woosley, Frieda C	Frieda C (Childress) Woosley
5	A-02-22a	[1866-1947]	Woosley, George Hopson	George Hopson Woosley
11	A-06-22	[1817-1892]	Woosley, George Washington	George Washington Woosley
38	B-05-12a	[1869-1958]	Woosley, George Washington	George Washington Woosley
5	A-03-02a	[1901-1998]	Woosley, Glida E	Glida E (Toms) Woosley
9	A-04-25	[1915-2002]	Woosley, Gracie	Gracie (Jones) Woosley
9	A-04-24	[1936-1936]	Woosley, Gracie Lee	Gracie Lee Woosley
27	A-19-19	[1838-1863]	Woosley, Greenville	Greenville Woosley
5	A-03-03	[1928-1928]	Woosley, Infant Daughter	Infant Daughter Woosley
24	A-17-27	[1867-1867]	Woosley, Infant Daughter	Infant Daughter Woosley
24	A-17-29	[1868-1868]	Woosley, Infant Daughter	Infant Daughter Woosley
26	A-18-15.12	[1884-1884]	Woosley, Infant Daughter	Infant Daughter Woosley
26	A-18-15c	[1808-1864]	Woosley, James Joseph B	James Joseph B Woosley
29	A-21-16	[1808-1864]	Woosley, James Joseph B	James Joseph B Woosley
7	A-03-27	[1874-1950]	Woosley, James Samuel	James Samuel Woosley
39	B-06-15b	[1902-1975]	Woosley, Jane L	Jane L (Woosley) Woosley
7	A-03-29	[1955-2001]	Woosley, Jannis Jann	Jannis Jann (Melton) Woosley
19	A-12-12	[1872-1875]	Woosley, Jasper T	Jasper T Woosley
39	B-06-09	[1948-1948]	Woosley, Jimmie Coleman	Jimmie Coleman Woosley
3	A-01-14a	[1860-1923]	Woosley, John Campbell Brackenridge	John Campbell Brackenridge Woosley
3	A-01-13	[1891-1899]	Woosley, John Jack	John Jack Woosley
4	A-02-19	[1833-1879]	Woosley, John Jack	John Jack Woosley
13	A-07-26b	[1843-1930]	Woosley, Joseph	Joseph Woosley
15	A-08-16a	[1884-1976]	Woosley, Judge Halsel	Judge Halsel Woosley
38	B-05-10a	[1929-2003]	Woosley, Kendall Sheridan	Kendall Sheridan Woosley
37	B-02-08a	[1905-1987]	Woosley, Kirby	Kirby Woosley
37	B-03-03a	[1912-2002]	Woosley, Landon	Landon Woosley
27	A-19-17	[1843-1922]	Woosley, Leah Lee	Leah Lee (Denton) Woosley
9	A-04-22	[1895-1962]	Woosley, Lester	Lester Woosley
9	A-04-28b	[1922-2000]	Woosley, Lester Avon	Lester Avon Woosley
26	A-18-15e	[1859-1931]	Woosley, Lewis Franklin	Lewis Franklin Woosley
4	A-02-17b	[1806-1954]	Woosley, Lewis Granville	Lewis Granville Woosley
39	B-06-15a	[1894-1963]	Woosley, Lewis Washington	Lewis Washington Woosley

38	B-04-13b	[1934-]	Woosley, Lillie E	Lillie E (Andersen) Woosley
7	A-03-28	[1901-1979]	Woosley, Linnie	Linnie (Gross) Woosley
8	A-04-21	[1895-1918]	Woosley, Luvenia Venia	Luvenia Venia (Raymer) Woosley
39	B-05-12b	[1884-1952]	Woosley, Margaret Maggie	Margaret Maggie (Burks) Woosley
9	A-04-30	[1963-1991]	Woosley, Mark L	Mark L Woosley
3	A-01-14b	[1866-1938]	Woosley, Martha Helen	Martha Helen (Woosley) Woosley
16	A-09-07b	[1887-1935]	Woosley, Martha Lee	Martha Lee (Woosley) Woosley
7	A-03-26	[1871-1924]	Woosley, Martha Thomas	Martha Thomas (Woosley) Woosley
20	A-12-13	[1868-1871]	Woosley, Mary E	Mary E Woosley
11	A-06-20a	[1840-1913]	Woosley, Mary Elizabeth	Mary Elizabeth (Simpson) Woosley
16	A-09-06b	[1846-1935]	Woosley, Mary Jane	Mary Jane (Brooks) Woosley
9	A-04-28a	[1917-1997]	Woosley, Mary L	Mary L (Semon) Woosley
36	B-02-01a	[1922-2007]	Woosley, McKelvy	McKelvy Woosley
15	A-08-16b	[1882-1931]	Woosley, Meda Meadie	Meda Meadie (Huff) Woosley
36	B-01-07b	[1963-2008]	Woosley, Melinda	Melinda (Huff) Woosley
11	A-06-20b	[1838-1906]	Woosley, Merrel	Merrel Woosley
22	A-15-16b	[1850-1922]	Woosley, Mildred Millie	Mildred Millie (Nash) Woosley
17	A-09-18a	[1882-1962]	Woosley, Minnie H	Minnie H (Huff) Woosley
13	A-07-24	[1879-1911]	Woosley, Minnie M	Minnie M (Huff) Woosley
37	B-02-10b	[1932-2009]	Woosley, Mona Laverne	Mona Laverne (Woosley) Woosley
38	B-05-10b	[1930-]	Woosley, Myra	Myra (Ellis) Woosley
19	A-12-11	[1840-1882]	Woosley, Nancy Jane	Nancy Jane (Oller) Woosley
11	A-06-19a	[1884-1945]	Woosley, Ollie Oscar	Ollie Oscar Woosley
11	A-06-18	[1914-1982]	Woosley, Raymond Leon	Raymond Leon Woosley
28	A-20-15	[1808-1890]	Woosley, Rebecca B	Rebecca B (Blakely) Woosley
30	A-21-23	[1851-1858]	Woosley, Robert A	Robert A Woosley
4	A-02-18	[1832-1892]	Woosley, Rosemon Rosie	Rosemon Rosie (Jones) Woosley
4	A-02-21	[1867-1896]	Woosley, Ruthy Addie	Ruthy Addie (Wells) Woosley
4	A-02-17a	[1867-1940]	Woosley, Samantha	Samantha (Huff) Woosley
16	A-09-06a	[1844-1923]	Woosley, Samuel	Samuel Woosley
28	A-20-16	[1802-1865]	Woosley, Samuel	Samuel Woosley
27	A-19-18	[1838-1905]	Woosley, Samuel M	Samuel M Woosley
37	B-03-03b	[1914-2000]	Woosley, Sedalia H	Sedalia H (Huff) Woosley
10	A-06-09	[1884-1888]	Woosley, Sherley	Sherley Woosley
16	A-09-08	[1917-1917]	Woosley, Shirley Gordon	Shirley Gordon Woosley
13	A-07-23	[1877-1944]	Woosley, Silas Calvin	Silas Calvin Woosley
22	A-15-16a	[1847-1914]	Woosley, Silas Calvin	Silas Calvin Woosley
11	A-06-26a	[1885-1954]	Woosley, Stella	Stella (Huff) Woosley
9	A-04-29	[1959-1977]	Woosley, Stephen Dale	Stephen Dale Woosley
13	A-07-26a	[1844-1924]	Woosley, Susan D	Susan D (Nash) Woosley
4	A-02-20a	[1869-1934]	Woosley, Susie Catherine	Susie Catherine (Woosley) Woosley
9	A-04-23	[1902-1953]	Woosley, Syble	Syble (Jones) Woosley
19	A-12-10	[1840-1919]	Woosley, Terrel	Terrel Woosley
11	A-06-26b	[1867-1946]	Woosley, Thomas J	Thomas J Woosley
28	A-20-14	[1840-1916]	Woosley, Thomas Jefferson	Thomas Jefferson Woosley
26	A-18-15.13	[1848-1848]	Woosley, Twin Boys	Twin Boys Woosley
21	A-13-09	[1889-1976]	Woosley, Valda	Valda Woosley
17	A-09-18b	[1873-1960]	Woosley, Volentine T	Volentine T Woosley
37	B-02-10a	[1929-2001]	Woosley, Wilcy	Wilcy Woosley
21	A-13-10	[1863-1902]	Woosley, William N	William N Woosley
13	A-07-22	[1898-1933]	Woosley, Zilpha	Zilpha (Nash) Woosley
10	A-06-12	[1857-1888]	Woosley, Zilphane M	Zilphane M (Anderson) Woosley

3 - UNKNOWNS

Page	Sect/Row/Plot	Dates	Surname	Full Name
6	A-03-16.01	[unk-unk]	Unknown A-03-16.01	Unknown A-03-16.01, Block Marker
6	A-03-16.02	[unk-unk]	Unknown A-03-16.02	Unknown A-03-16.02, Field Stone Marker
7	A-04-05	[unk-unk]	Unknown A-04-05	Unknown A-04-05, White Marker
7	A-04-08	[unk-unk]	Unknown A-04-08	Unknown A-04-08, White Marker
9	A-05-09	[unk-unk]	Unknown A-05-09	Unknown A-05-09, White D. W. Marker
10	A-06-08	[unk-unk]	Unknown A-06-08	Unknown A-06-08, Illegible Headstone Marker
11	A-06-17b.01	[unk-unk]	Unknown A-06-17b.01	Unknown A-06-17b.01, White S.A.D.. Marker
11	A-06-23	[unk-unk]	Unknown A-06-23	Unknown A-06-23, Illegible White Stone Marker
11	A-06-24	[unk-unk]	Unknown A-06-24	Unknown A-06-24, Illegible White Stone Marker
12	A-07-05	[unk-unk]	Unknown A-07-05	Unknown A-07-05, Willis Stone Broken
14	A-08-01	[unk-unk]	Unknown A-08-01	Unknown A-08-01, Illegible White Stone Marker
15	A-08-23	[unk-unk]	Unknown A-08-23	Unknown A-08-23, Field Stone Marker
16	A-08-24	[unk-unk]	Unknown A-08-24	Unknown A-08-24, Broken Stone Marker
16	A-08-25	[unk-unk]	Unknown A-08-25	Unknown A-08-25, Field Stone Marker
20	A-12-16	[unk-unk]	Unknown A-12-16	Unknown A-12-16, Field Stone Marker
20	A-12-17	[unk-unk]	Unknown A-12-17	Unknown A-12-17, Field Stone Marker
20	A-12-27	[unk-unk]	Unknown A-12-27	Unknown A-12-27, Illegible Stone Marker
21	A-13-21	[unk-unk]	Unknown A-13-21	Unknown A-13-21, Field Stone Marker
23	A-16-26	[unk-unk]	Unknown A-16-26	Unknown A-16-26, Field Stone Marker
24	A-16-40	[unk-unk]	Unknown A-16-40	Unknown A-16-40, Stone Marker
25	A-18-08	[unk-unk]	Unknown A-18-08	Unknown A-18-08, Field Stone Marker
25	A-18-09	[unk-unk]	Unknown A-18-09	Unknown A-18-09, Field Stone Marker
25	A-18-10	[unk-unk]	Unknown A-18-10	Unknown A-18-10, Field Stone Marker
25	A-18-13	[unk-unk]	Unknown A-18-13	Unknown A-18-13, Field Stone Marker
25	A-18-14	[unk-unk]	Unknown A-18-14	Unknown A-18-14, Field Stone Marker
25	A-18-15	[unk-unk]	Unknown A-18-15.00	Unknown A-18-15.00, Field Stone Marker
27	A-19-10	[unk-unk]	Unknown A-19-10	Unknown A-19-10, Field Stone Marker
27	A-19-11	[unk-unk]	Unknown A-19-11	Unknown A-19-11, Field Stone Marker
27	A-19-12	[unk-unk]	Unknown A-19-12	Unknown A-19-12, Field Stone Marker
27	A-19-13	[unk-unk]	Unknown A-19-13	Unknown A-19-13, Field Stone Marker
27	A-19-14	[unk-unk]	Unknown A-19-14	Unknown A-19-14, Field Stone Marker
27	A-19-15	[unk-unk]	Unknown A-19-15	Unknown A-19-15, Field Stone Marker
27	A-19-16	[unk-unk]	Unknown A-19-16	Unknown A-19-16, Field Stone Marker
27	A-19-20	[unk-unk]	Unknown A-19-20	Unknown A-19-20, Field Stone Marker
27	A-19-21	[unk-unk]	Unknown A-19-21	Unknown A-19-21, Field Stone Marker
27	A-19-22	[unk-unk]	Unknown A-19-22	Unknown A-19-22, Field Stone Marker
27	A-19-23	[unk-unk]	Unknown A-19-23	Unknown A-19-23, Field Stone Marker
28	A-19-29	[unk-unk]	Unknown A-19-29	Unknown A-19-29, Field Stone Marker
28	A-20-06	[unk-unk]	Unknown A-20-06	Unknown A-20-06, S. W. Stone Marker
28	A-20-08	[unk-unk]	Unknown A-20-08	Unknown A-20-08, Field Stone Marker
28	A-20-09	[unk-unk]	Unknown A-20-09	Unknown A-20-09, Field Stone Marker
28	A-20-21	[unk-unk]	Unknown A-20-21	Unknown A-20-21, Field Stone Marker
29	A-20-39	[unk-unk]	Unknown A-20-39	Unknown A-20-39, Field Stone Marker
30	A-21-32	[unk-unk]	Unknown A-21-32	Unknown A-21-32, Field Stone Marker
30	A-21-34	[unk-unk]	Unknown A-21-34	Unknown A-21-34, RBE Stone Marker
31	A-22-18	[unk-unk]	Unknown A-22-18	Unknown A-22-18, Field Stone Marker
31	A-22-26	[unk-unk]	Unknown A-22-26	Unknown A-22-26, Field Stone Marker
31	A-22-27	[unk-unk]	Unknown A-22-27	Unknown A-22-27, Field Stone Marker
31	A-22-28	[unk-unk]	Unknown A-22-28	Unknown A-22-28, Field Stone Marker
31	A-22-31	[unk-unk]	Unknown A-22-31	Unknown A-22-31, Field Stone Marker
31	A-22-32	[unk-unk]	Unknown A-22-32	Unknown A-22-32, Block Marker
32	A-23-25	[unk-unk]	Unknown A-23-25	Unknown A-23-25, Field Stone Marker
32	A-23-26	[unk-unk]	Unknown A-23-26	Unknown A-23-26, Field Stone Marker
32	A-23-28	[unk-unk]	Unknown A-23-28	Unknown A-23-28, Field Stone Marker
32	A-23-31	[unk-unk]	Unknown A-23-31	Unknown A-23-31, Field Stone Marker
33	A-24-18	[unk-unk]	Unknown A-24-18	Unknown A-24-18, Field Stone Marker
33	A-24-21	[unk-unk]	Unknown A-24-21	Unknown A-24-21, Field Stone Marker
33	A-24-22	[unk-unk]	Unknown A-24-22	Unknown A-24-22, Field Stone Marker
33	A-24-29	[unk-unk]	Unknown A-24-29	Unknown A-24-29, Illegible Headstone Marker
33	A-24-31a	[unk-unk]	Unknown A-24-31a	Unknown A-24-31a, Field Stone Marker
33	A-24-31b	[unk-unk]	Unknown A-24-31b	Unknown A-24-31b, Field Stone Marker
34	A-26-22	[unk-unk]	Unknown A-24-22	Unknown A-24-22, Field Stone Marker
34	A-26-24	[unk-unk]	Unknown A-26-24	Unknown A-26-24, V L White Stone Marker

Page	Sect/Row/Plot	Dates	Surname	Full Name
35	A-26-31	[unk-unk]	Unknown A-26-31	Unknown A-26-31, Illegible White Stone Marker
35	A-27-19	[unk-unk]	Unknown A-27-19	Unknown A-27-19, L. L. S. White Stone Marker
35	A-27-24	[unk-unk]	Unknown A-27-24	Unknown A-27-24, Illegible White Stone Marker
35	A-27-26	[unk-unk]	Unknown A-27-26	Unknown A-27-26, Illegible White Stone Marker
35	A-27-31	[unk-unk]	Unknown A-27-31	Unknown A-27-31, Illegible White Stone Marker
38	B-06-11	[unk-unk]	Unknown B-06-11	Unknown B-06-11, C.W.W. reserved Marker
38	B-06-12	[unk-unk]	Unknown B-06-12	Unknown B-06-12, D.R.D. reserved Marker
38	B-06-13	[unk-unk]	Unknown B-06-13	Unknown B-06-13, S.C.D. reserved Marker

ABOUT THE AUTHOR

Daniel Durbin was born in a very small town in southern Kentucky, but was primarily raised in Louisville. He holds a Bachelor's Degree in Computer Science and is a Vietnam Era Combat Veteran. After multiple successful careers he officially "retired" in 2013.

Daniel is a published author with seven books to his credit since retirement. A saga of early childhood, biography of his time in the Army during the Vietnam Era, and multiple genealogy books are now behind him.

Genealogy was always a sideline hobby through the last 40 plus years. Retirement has offered the opportunity to pursue this hobby with renewed vigor. The importance of recording for posterity the ancestors that preceded us carries a special meaning for Daniel. "If we do not know where we came from how can we expect to get where we are going?"